SUPERSTITION
or
SCIENTIFIC FACT?

Most people laugh at ghost stories nowadays—we "know there's nothing in it." Yet, throughout history, and in our own time, sober, responsible people have braved ridicule to give sworn accounts of

> ghosts
> prophetic dreams
> telepathy
> clairvoyance
> poltergeists

and other "impossible" phenomena. And now, in research institutions the world over, scientific experiments are being conducted—testing **and proving** the validity of so-called "supernatural" manifestations.

Susy Smith, a well-known authority in the field of psychic research, here discusses the long history of supernormal happenings, and reveals the exciting discoveries of today's researchers.

ESP

BY
SUSY
SMITH

PYRAMID BOOKS ▲ NEW YORK

Dedicated to H. Wm. (Bill) Hane-
mann of Daytona Beach, Florida, an
editor of value beyond ivory, apes,
and peacocks.

E S P

A Pyramid Book

First printing, October 1962

Pyramid Books *are published by Pyramid Publications, Inc.,
444 Madison Avenue, New York 22, New York, U.S.A.*

Contents

Introduction

"Extrasensory Perceptions" is the formidable-sounding name currently applied to occurrences of various queer kinds—clairvoyance, precognition, telepathy, and certain others—of which instances have occasionally been reported from all parts of the world throughout history.

In an article on "The Relevance of Psychical Research to Philosophy" published some years ago, however, the eminent Cambridge University philosopher Professor C. D. Broad pointed out that those occurrences, if real, would definitely clash with "certain limiting principles which we unhesitatingly take for granted as the framework within which all our practical activities and our scientific theories are confined."

This clash is the reason why the great majority of scientists today question or deny outright that occurrences of the odd kinds in view ever really take place.

In the present work, Miss Smith addresses herself to the question on the answer to which the validity of this verdict wholly rests; the question, namely, whether those limiting principles are themselves valid not only, as we know, very widely, but valid without any exceptions at all.

She reviews the various kinds of evidence now available that exceptions to them do sometimes occur; that is, that some genuine cases of clairvoyance, of telepathy, and of the other kinds of extrasensory perception really exist. She considers the history of the study of the subject, and various of the far-reaching implications brought to light by the attempt to carry on that study in a strictly scientific manner.

Moreover, the answers she reports and discusses, to the fascinating question she chose as title for the book, are not only documented interestingly throughout, but are presented with the lucidity and in the engaging style which readers of Miss Smith's earlier writings have come to expect.

The book is an exceptionally readable and informing introduction to a subject the importance of which is now receiving increasingly wide recognition.

C. J. Ducasse
Brown University

1 *Introducing ESP*

voices. St. Teresa of Avila begged her sister nuns to sit on her so she wouldn't float in the air. Mark Twain saw his brother in his coffin shortly before he was killed in a steamboat accident on the Mississippi. Emmanuel Swedenborg described the leaping flames of a great fire as it burned in Stockholm, although he was in Gottenberg, three hundred miles away.

Certain people are more likely than others to have such unusual experiences. They are called "psychics."

When someone seems to read our mind, and tells us what we have been thinking before we have put it into words, we say half-jestingly, "You must be psychic." But what do we mean? What do we imply when we say the same of Joan of Arc, St. Teresa, Mark Twain, and Swedenborg?

Usually our only contact with the world outside ourselves is through our five senses. If we can't see a thing, touch it, taste it, smell or hear it, we're satisfied that it isn't there. Yet all through history there have been persistent indications that knowledge can be acquired supernormally.

It is with what is considered to be supernormal that this book is concerned: extrasensory perception—the acquisition of knowledge that is extra or beyond the scope of the senses with which we are familiar. It will be shown that such occurrences—known as psychic—may not be as much beyond the normal as we think and that perhaps it is our knowledge of what is normal that must be broadened.

9

Introducing ESP

We dream that a relative has been injured in an automobile accident and hear the next morning that during the night he *was* injured in an automobile accident. Perhaps this is chance or coincidence. But if the attendant details of our dream match exactly those which really occurred, then we should suspect that the information about the accident came to us extra-sensorilly.

Pearl Buck gives us an instance of information supernormally acquired, in her book *A Bridge for Passing*.* She opened her eyes in a Tokyo hotel at five o'clock one morning, wide awake, alarmed by something intangible, unknown. "I lay motionless in my bed," she says, "listening, waiting, convinced that someone was trying to reach me."

At a quarter to six the telephone rang, and she knew immediately what it was—her daughter calling from the States to tell her that her husband, chronically ill for the past six years, had just died.

Singer Tito Scipa stopped at an inn in Vercelli, Italy where he made his debut in *Traviata*. But instead of the proverbial jovial host, he found only a gloomy innkeeper's eldest son, who had not inherited from his father as he had expected, because his father's will could not be found. The inn was soon to be sold to satisfy the heirs.

That night Scipa slept like a log, although the room he had been given was the one in which the innkeeper had died. The next night, however, the singer was less fortunate. He was awakened by a whirring noise as if some bird or bat had come in through the open window and was circling just above his head in the direction of the left wall. He got up and searched the room, but found nothing. His fitful sleep was later disturbed by the sound of words spoken almost inaudibly: "Look on the left wall."

This Scipa did, but saw nothing. He climbed back into bed; but his annoyance was to continue, so he finally de-

*The John Day Co., Inc., New York, 1961.

cided to investigate the persistent left wall thoroughly. Dragging a table across the floor, he climbed up on it, and took down an old oil painting hanging there, in case a bat might be caught behind it. As he handled the picture the gleam of white paper caught his eye. Scipa says:* "It was neatly folded and stuck at the back of the picture between a wooden stretcher and the canvas. Pulling the paper out, I took it to the window to investigate. It was the lost will, leaving the inn to the writer's eldest son."

Instances such as these are not as rare as might be thought. They are happening around the world all the time. The fact that they are indifferently reported, if at all, does not make them any the less true. When they are viewed in the aggregate their significance is apparent. There is a great deal in our universe of which we know very little and we are barely beginning to be aware of it.

During the past few decades, because of the advances in science, man has had to change much of his thinking about almost everything. One of the main areas in which the biggest change has occurred is in his ideas concerning the fundamental nature of his own mind.

Oddly enough, with all that we know about the *brain,* the *mind* is a subject about which very little has ever been really ascertained. Science has never been able to tell us exactly what the mind is, what thought is, what consciousness is. In the past this lack of knowledge has always been more or less disregarded, as we accepted certain vague beliefs which covered the subject adequately enough for our purposes.

It was commonly maintained for many centuries that man consisted of a body, a mind, and a soul. The soul was spiritual and the body material. The consciousness, or mind, of man, cooperating with the soul, enjoyed free will and could control the body. This belief sustained the deeply religious and those who do not readily accept new

Philadelphia Public Ledger, February 12, 1928.

doctrines; but with the late 19th Century came Materialism—the theory that matter is the only reality.

We began to believe that we were controlled by the inexorable operation of mechanical law; that an endless chain of cause and effect governed our lives; that the only occurrences that ultimately counted in determining behavior were bodily ones, for all mental activity was dependent upon the physical function of the body.

Psychiatry came into its own. Freud and his followers, behavior-oriented, convinced us that childhood experiences and emotions were the controlling factors in our lives, and "free-will" fell by the wayside.

Then we split the atom. And we are having once again to change our ideas. For it was discovered that the atom is mostly an empty hole, and thus that everything formerly considered to be solid matter is actually almost entirely composed of space. The rest of it is some force analogous to electricity.

Many of our current scientific thinkers of great stature have expressed themselves publicly about the pure enigmas arising from the splitting of the atom and the dissolution of matter, and about the necessity for us to revamp and reshape our thinking to meet these new concepts. Among these men are Erwin Schröedinger, Max Planck, Niels Bohr, Henry Margenau, Edmund Sinnott, and Albert Einstein himself. But the one who seems to have stated it most clearly for our present needs is Donald Hatch Andrews of the Department of Chemistry, Johns Hopkins University.

Dr. Andrews tells us that if the body of a man were condensed in a press which could squeeze out all the space in all its atoms, like squeezing out the holes of a sponge, to the point where it was pure solid matter and no holes, it would be smaller than the tiniest speck of dust which one could see lying on a sheet of paper.

"In fact," Dr. Andrews says, "with such an atomic press

one could squeeze down the entire human race, every man, woman and child on earth, to the point where they could all be put in a bottle which you could slip right in your pocket. That shows how little we amount to in a material way."

Dr. Andrews goes on that, "If the atom is really mostly empty space filled with a little electricity, and only a tiny speck of matter at its center [and matter itself is actually only waves or vibrations], we have to revise our ideas about what is real. It is clear that we can no longer take our senses as our guides. When my finger touches a piece of wood it is not *matter* touching *matter;* it is an *electrical wave* touching another *electrical wave*. When I look at you, I am not seeing matter; I am seeing a harmonic complex of electrical vibration. And what is more important, I am seeing far less than one percent of all the vibration which you are producing. For your presence is manifested far more in the invisible world than in the visible. And to understand your *total* reality we must examine this world of invisible vibrations and invisible forces."

Among these forces are gravity, the thousands of electrical waves which are the carriers of radio programs from all over the world, which are passing right through us every instant, and a sea of infra red or thermal waves. Dr. Andrews says that, "The atoms in our bodies are giving off radiation of this kind all the time. When we meet, you radiate infra red at me; I radiate it back at you. Every muscle movement, every nerve impulse, every thought results in some wave of this sort." There are also the ultra violet rays from the sun, x-rays, and the gamma rays from decomposing atoms; and finally there are the cosmic rays, those mysterious messengers which come flying in to us all the time from outer space.

At this moment, according to Dr. Andrews, cosmic radiation is streaming right down through the roof over your head, passing through your body, passing down through the floor, and finally burying itself, lost in the earth beneath. What role these cosmic rays play in the life process we do not yet know. We live and move in a world of invisible forces.

Yet even though it can now be said that modern physics has dematerialized matter—if you walk into a table you still get a bruise. Familiar substances such as wood, water, air, and living bodies still have the properties we perceive them to have. What physics has shown is that there is much *more* to everything than we perceive. We have been awakened to the fact that the five senses with which each individual has contact with the world about him do not show him *all* of the world, but only limited aspects of it. In the area of sight alone we know that it is possible for man to see only a very limited portion of the light spectrum. In the realm of sound we have discovered that dogs respond to high-pitched whistles that the human ear is incapable of hearing.

So from the viewpoint of ordinary sensory perception man is becoming aware that he knows considerably less than he suspected about the universe. Must we then continue to insist that things do not exist merely because we cannot see them, hear them, touch, taste or smell them? In a world which has split the atom, certainly not.

Now we don't have to think of man in terms of purely physical and chemical processes, as the mechanistic theory has so long held. Now we can more readily accept an idea of man which may be contrary to what we previously believed to be true. Now we are at a stage in our thinking in which we are more prepared to take seriously the subject of *extra*-sensory perception.

2 *What Is Extrasensory Perception?*

THROUGHOUT THE world in all ages and times certain persons have been able to produce supernormal phenomena and to acquire knowledge by other means than the normal data provided by their known senses. These individuals have been esteemed as prophets, oracles, or medicine men, or else feared as witches or sorcerers, associates of the Devil to be despised and persecuted.

Up until the last two and a half centuries almost everyone took paranormal manifestations for granted and accepted them as evidence of either good or evil, definitely a part of their lives, not to be questioned. But in recent times, the development of the scientific method of observation has led us to discredit people with psychic talents, as it tends to discount effects for which causes cannot be determined. As there is no mechanistic explanation for their unaccountable activities, these were thought to be neither important nor true. The majority of authoritative scientists have considered the reports of psychic experiences to be no more than the result of superstition, imagination, coincidence, bad memory, or faulty observation on the part of highly emotional persons. Which, to be sure, they could on many occasions have been.

But in examining the accounts of psychic occurrences, we always discover certain instances so well witnessed and so thoroughly documented that only an uninformed or arrantly stubborn person could refuse to recognize them as something beyond the normal.

Those who make it their business to investigate such cases and to try to learn the whys and wherefores of these capacities are called psychical researchers, or, more com-

15

monly now, parapsychologists. They have collected and
analyzed a vast quantity of case histories of personal
supernormal experiences which by its sheer mass is
impressive.

Extrasensory perception—information gained without
the use of the senses—is an integral part of this psychic
field. Hunches, intuition, premonitions, and other experiences of everyday life belong under the heading of extrasensory perception *if* they bring real knowledge without
sensory means. It is never knowledge which could come by
mental processes such as memory, reasoning, inference, or
guessing. Extrasensory experiences occur to some people
spontaneously when least expected; they occur frequently
to some highly psychic persons; and they may on occasion
be induced experimentally in a laboratory. Dr. J. B.
Rhine's work at the Parapsychology Laboratory at Duke
University is the most familiar to Americans.

There are two main underlying characteristics that can
be observed in all ESP experiences. The first is that
psychic events are not impersonal, such as an imminent
earthquake; they are always linked to people. The second
is that they are not merely unexplainable; they seem down-
right impossible in the light of our present knowledge. In
most cases we are strongly tempted to doubt that they
could have happened at all, no matter how good the
testimony may be, because we are aware of no natural
laws to explain them. There is no reasonable way that we
know of by which they could have been produced.

Extrasensory phenomena of this nature used to be
stowed in three handy separate compartments: telepathy,
clairvoyance, and precognition. Telepathy was defined as
extrasensory awareness of another person's thoughts, or
the passing of information from one to another without
ordinary means of communication. For instance, if I look
at the queen of spades which is hidden from you, and you

16

tell me that the card I am looking at is the queen of spades, this is *telepathy* in action.

When the idea of telepathy was first conceived, back in the latter part of the last century, it was believed that some kind of thought transference from one mind to another was always involved in psychic experiences. Psychical researchers began to realize, however, that just as often, in both spontaneous and experimental cases, there was the possibility that contact was made not between one mind and another, but between a mind and an object. This, then, came to be called *clairvoyance*. In our illustration this time I will not look at the face of the card, but will pull it from the deck and lay it in front of me face down. Now neither of us knows what the card is. If you then tell me it is the queen of spades, and we both look and discover that this is true, clairvoyance on your part is indicated.

Very often individuals seem to be able to predict the future. This is called *precognition*. Using our deck of cards once more, you tell me where a specific card will fall in the deck after it is shuffled. You say that the queen of spades will be the third card from the top. I then shuffle the deck carefully many times and cut it often. I do not allow you to touch it, for although I know you are honest, I don't want anyone else to be able to suggest that you might have practiced sleight of hand. Then we look at the third card from the top and it is the queen of spades. Precognition.

Where precognition is in evidence, there may also be other ESP as well. In cases indicating telepathy or clairvoyance, especially those occurring spontaneously, it is particularly difficult to make a clear cut distinction. And so a fourth category called *general extrasensory perception*, or GESP, has come to be acknowledged. Parapsychologists actually aren't greatly concerned about which word to use to classify the experience, unless they are giving tests for a certain type in a laboratory. It seems more important to them to discuss its authenticity, how well-attested it is, and the likelihood of chance being involved.

It will be seen in the following examples of psychic (or psi) experiences how difficult it would be to classify each case as one specific type of ESP, for it could be either telepathy or clairvoyance; and in the first case there is even an element of precognition.

Mrs. R. B. Storrs of Birmingham, Alabama wrote to the American Society for Psychical Research in March, 1957 that two years before her parents had gone on a short vacation. When about seventy-six miles away from home they stopped at a place where there was no telephone. Mrs. Storrs' mother, Mrs. Velma C. Vann, had a dream that night in which she discovered the Storrs' little son Bobby to be extremely ill, burning with fever. Mrs. Vann dreamed she picked him up, and she says,* "While I was sitting there rocking Bobby I was crying because he seemed almost dead. My son Bud came to the door of Bobby's room and leaned up against the door frame with his hand to his head. I asked him what was wrong and he said he fell from a telephone pole." Mrs. Vann then saw in her dream that her son Bud had a vicious gash just above his eye, from which blood was pouring.

Frightened by her dream, Mrs. Vann and her husband returned home immediately. There they discovered little Bobby to be very ill with a high fever. While they were discussing his condition with his mother, Bud, a lineman for the telephone company, walked in holding his head and bleeding profusely from a cut he had received when he fell from a telephone pole.

The following case seems to be more indicative of telep-

*"A Selection of Cases from a Recent Survey of Spontaneous ESP Phenomena" by Laura A. Dale, Rhea White, and Gardner Murphy, The *Journal* of the American Society for Psychical Research, Vol. LVI, No. 1, January, 1962.

athy, and yet clairvoyance must not be entirely ruled out, for it could play its part here too:

On March 18, 1955 Mrs. R. J. Russell of Rochester, Indiana had a sudden desperate need for a small amount of money. She was sure that $10 or $15 would be ample to cover her situation. Although she had never appealed to her daughters before for financial assistance, and hated to ask for it, on this occasion she sat down and wrote to her daughter, Mrs. Aileen Smithwick, asking for $10.

Mrs. Smithwick, a registered nurse who has had many ESP experiences, was on a vacation in Las Vegas, Nevada. On the night of March 18th she was in bed, drowsy and relaxed, but unable to fall asleep. She sensed a message from her mother in Indiana that she needed either $10 or $15. In her letter to the American Society for Psychical Research Mrs. Smithwick says* she felt the impression so strongly that:

> I got out of bed at the hotel, wrote the check, and went down and mailed it, with a sigh of relief. I promptly went back to bed and forgot it. When I returned home a few days later, I found a letter from my mother asking me for $10.

The letter was dated the exact day and hour that the daughter was so disturbed. Later, in discussing it, they both learned that the sum of $15 had been thought of by the other, although in both cases the lesser amount was decided upon.

Now this sounds like a good story, but is it true? In order that an incident of this nature may be considered veridical, corroborating testimony is essential. In this case we have a letter from Mrs. Smithwick's sister, Mrs. Elizabeth Oswald, stating that her mother had told her of her surprise at receiving Aileen's check before the letter asking for it could have reached her. In addition we have

Ibid.

Mrs. Smithwick's cancelled check payable to Mrs. Russell in the amount of $10 dated March 18, 1955.

Engaging the attention of psychical researchers are many other evidences of psi so closely allied to ESP that it is difficult to separate them completely. These, which will be discussed more fully in subsequent chapters, include ghosts and poltergeists, and out-of-body experiences, or astral projections, where a person seems actually to leave his body and travel about. Psychokinesis, the effect of mind over matter, will be gone into, along with the tests for it at Duke University, which have shown that the throw of dice can be mentally controlled.

Among other things to be disclosed are:

The strange states produced by hallucinogenic drugs.

Levitation, the ability possessed by a few persons to raise their bodies into the air. It sounds even wilder than most of these tales; but there have been several instances of levitation which are well-enough attested to make psychical researchers take it seriously, although they haven't yet been able to explain it.

The word Spiritualism to many people carries connotations of "gullibility," because this religion acknowledges that communication is possible with souls who have survived bodily death. It is safe to say that many Spiritualists *are* gullible, and believe anything they hear, no matter how fictitious or fraudulent it may be. Yet over the years material has been received in churches of this denomination which is definitely supernormal. If the spirit hypothesis is not accepted, then the information which allegedly comes from spirits should be attributed to a very high order of ESP.

Those who believe that communication with surviving spirits has been proved, in the light of what they consider to be unassailable scientific evidence, are called spiritists. Many of the greatest psychical researchers, skeptical at the beginning of their investigations, have ultimately been convinced after years of work that communication is possible. But very few of them have accepted Spiritualism as a religion.

The study of mediumship is a function of parapsychology. If material received by mediums does not come from spirits it must come from some extrasensory source, unless the medium practices deception, and this is unfortunately sometimes the case. We will discuss the possible reasons for this later, in the chapter on the Problems of Mediumship.

3   *Who Has ESP?*

giving it little consideration, most people seem to have
extrasensory perception in dilute form. A letter from a
remote friend of whom you dreamed the night before is
dismissed as common coincidence. Knowing what others
are going to ask before they ask it or who is on the telephone before lifting the receiver appears a little more unusual. Deliberately drawing, against better judgment, to
an inside straight and getting away with it invites momen-
tary pause and wonder. When these isolated instances
appear frequently, they are more than chance. If your
hunches are repeatedly successful, if your "coincidences"
become daily affairs, you might as well face the fact that
you are psychic. You are, whether it pleases you or not,
"sensitive" to paranormal impressions.

In their book, *The Unknown—Is It Nearer?*, Eric J.
Dingwall and John Langdon-Davies tell us that their collected evidence indicates that "everybody has ESP, but in
most people it has been completely repressed in favor of
normal means of perception." Certain individuals, they
believe, are more likely than others to allow bits of their
ESP to escape from time to time, functioning only in
certain moods. If the mood is destroyed, the ESP goes
with it. Overanxiety, overeagerness, lack of confidence, or
plain boredom readily dispel the favorable conditions as
well as do the wrong sort of surroundings. Relaxed, half-
asleep, or suddenly stimulated by the excitement of a
critical situation, these sensitives produce definite and
highly engrossing phenomena.

Sigmund Freud has said of telepathy* that "one is led

*New Introductory Lectures on Psychoanalysis, London, Hogarth Press, 1934.

22

to conjecture that [it] may be the original archaic method by which individuals understood one another." The evolution of a better means of communication by signs intelligible to the sense organs, Freud speculates, pushed the older methods into the background where they may still persist to manifest themselves under certain conditions.

Dr. J. B. Rhine is also inclined to favor this hypothesis. Extrasensory perception, he believes, might well have predated the origin, "not merely of language and of reason, but even of the sensory functions themselves."

Whether ESP is primitive or otherwise, ever since the general public has been aware of the activity of the Parapsychology Laboratory, it has been writing to North Carolina, eager to tell about paranormal experiences and to ask questions. Since so little is commonly known about psi (another word for psychic power), many who have occasionally to contend with it are puzzled and write to ask "what happened?" Dr. Louisa E. Rhine, wife of J. B. Rhine, speaks in her book, *Hidden Channels of the Mind*,* of the kind of people who write to them at Duke.

"The letters came, it appears," says Mrs. Rhine, "from the 'high' and the lowly, the rich and the poor, the obviously well-educated and those who, often by their own account, had little formal schooling. But of whatever background, it seemed that, just as a patient might tell his doctor his symptoms as clearly and factually as he could, so these people were trying to give a careful account of the events that had puzzled them. Their motives and intentions, in fact, seemed curiously uniform considering the diversity of individual backgrounds and kinds of experience.

"Although many individuals seemed hesitant and even a bit apologetic to be writing about a personal matter and admitting that such an inexplicable thing should have happened to them (many said in effect, 'If someone else had

---

*William Sloane Associates, New York, 1961.

told this to me I wouldn't have believed it'), perhaps the most frequently expressed motive for writing, in literally thousands of letters, was, 'I hope this will help in your researches.' "

So we see that a fair cross-sampling of those who have ESP shows them to be average, unpretentious citizens, who are just as surprised as anybody when they suddenly have a psychic experience. Even if extrasensory perception is a rudimentary method of communication, there is no indication that it is characteristic of subnormal mentality. Half-wit or egg head, ESP plays no favorites.

Children, in many cases, appear to be psychic, but these traits when repressed and rejected by unsympathetic adults are for the most part overlooked and outgrown. Dr. Louisa Rhine tells of two small boys in Illinois, one-and-a-half-year-old Chris and three-and-a-half-year-old Vic. The mother had left the younger child asleep at his grandmother's, a block and a half away. She says that in about forty-five minutes "Vic began to run to the window looking down the street and calling frantically to me that Chris was crying. . . I told Vic he was mistaken and went on with my work. He was very persistent and burst into tears, 'Chris wants you Mommie.' "

In about five minutes the grandmother arrived with a tearful Chris, saying that he had awakened sobbing for "Mommy" at two-ten, the exact time Vic had reported his distress.

Dr. Louisa Rhine also tells about a Wisconsin family returning home from a trip "when the four-year-old in the back seat stood up unexpectedly and asked, 'Did Aunt Myrtle and Uncle Charles have a wreck with a train?'

"The father in a disgusted tone asked, 'What are you talking about?' The answer, 'I see'd they did.'

"The next day word was received that the aunt and uncle had stalled their car on a railroad crossing. They had gotten out of it before a train hit and demolished the car. As far as could be estimated, it was at the time of the child's remark."

Twins have shown an unusually high telepathic rapport. Dr. Robert Sommer, psychologist at the University of Alberta, Canada, and his associates, British psychiatrist Dr. Humphry Osmond and research assistant Lucille Pancyr, have made a study of ESP in twins. Their results confirm a fact long suspected by parapsychologists: identical twins, and to a lesser extent, fraternal twins, have unusual ability to communicate with one another through extrasensory perception.

Dr. Sommer's recently published scientific report on twins and ESP is discussed in an article entitled "Can Twins Read Each Others' Minds?" by Jhan and June Robbins.* "One thing we have learned," says Dr. Sommer via the article, "is that two people who share an emotional closeness are more likely to report more successful ESP experiences than two strangers.

"Identical twins obviously share the closest possible relationship that can embrace two human beings. They actually started out as a single individual—and they have the same mental and physical attributes."

Dr. Sommer and his associates contacted twins in the Canadian city of Saskatoon who were willing to participate in the experiments. There were 35 of them—18 men and 17 women. There were 14 pairs of twins and seven twins where only one of a pair was available. Their ages ranged from 16 to 50. A twenty-seven-item scientifically designed interview disclosed that one-third of the twins had had paranormal experiences with their "other halves." These twins tended to be the ones who had always shared strong mutual interests and similar abilities.

The article goes on: "The Canada-based researchers are the first to undertake a full, scientific field study of a

This Week Magazine, January 28, 1962.

phenomenon that has long amazed the families and friends of twins. Recently, for example, a pair of lively 13-year olds in Jackson, Mississippi have been making headlines because of their apparent ability to communicate with one another without speaking a word. They are Sherry and Terry Young. They amuse their friends, puzzle their parents and often exasperate their teachers with their telepathic tricks.

" 'We believed that twins should spend some time apart,' their mother explained. 'We often sent one or the other to spend a night at their grandmother's house. But whenever one of the girls would turn her ankle, get a toothache, or develop a headache, the other would know it.'

"At school, teachers suspected that the two girls might be giving one another too much help. They put them in different classrooms, but the twins still received the same marks. The girls freely admitted that they 'helped' one another by telepathy."

Other twins have reported unanticipated experiences with telepathy and clairvoyance, Jhan and June (the assonance of whose names suggests they might be twins themselves, although they are actually a husband and wife writing team) continue:

"The father of 16-year-old twin girls in Indiana wrote us about the 'sixth-sense qualities' of his daughters. Once they had decided to go to a local carnival on alternate nights. On the night Della went, Stella was at home leaning over the ironing board, annoyed because she had burned her hand with the iron.

"Suddenly she felt a 'cold cloud' of terror descend on her. It was followed swiftly by a feeling of dizziness and nausea. She put aside her iron and walked rapidly to the fair grounds. There she learned that the Ferris wheel was stalled. Her sister, frightened and motion-sick, was swaying back and forth in the topmost car. When Della got down safely, two hours later, she flung her arms around Stella and exclaimed, 'You burned yourself again! Won't you ever learn how to iron?' "

As has been indicated, ESP is frequently an undeveloped power. With just the merest encouragement it might produce highly significant results. The late Professor James Hyslop of Columbia University told about a remarkable young lady of the best finishing-school tradition who, with very little training, might have become one of the most important and valuable psychic personalities. But her wealthy socialite parents strenuously objected. They would not hear of it! They did not want their daughter to have any traffic with spooks; and they feared for her social future if it should become known that she was in any way peculiar or different. In a word, they rejected their daughter's rare psychic gift, considering it in the light of a dreadful inheritance or a disgraceful disease.

We must sympathize with this young lady of Dr. Hyslop's, who might have won historical recognition in psychical circles as the possessor of such a great talent, yet we understand from those who have gone through life with such unsought largesse that existence can frequently be highly complicated because of it. Mrs. Helen Simpson Phillips of Front Royal, Virginia is one who for many years regretted having unusual psychic powers. A former head nurse at Mt. Sinai Hospital in New York City, Mrs. Phillips now knows that she has a gift shared by relatively few; but for the most of her life she believed it to be considerably less than a blessing. To her it was actually a curse, for she felt it set her apart. Those who knew of her psi looked upon her as a curiosity. She disliked the derision, the skepticism, or the gaping wonder which her curious ability so frequently aroused; and she usually tried not to let others know about it if she could help it.

Yet on occasion she had to give people the benefit of her super-knowledge. When the porter at her apartment

building lamented losing his master key and Helen could
plainly see it, lodged under a certain chip in a certain
woodpile, naturally she had to tell him. But when the
porter then pointed her out as "the lady who found my key
by seeing a picture of it inside her own head," she felt
thoroughly undignified and uncomfortable.

Yet, certainly it has its compensations. Most of us
would probably be willing to be pointed out as "different"
in order to be able to recover lost articles as Mrs. Phillips
can.

"Once when I lived in a nurses' home I left my watch
in the lavatory," she confided. "And when I remembered
and went back for it an hour later, it was gone. Dozens of
girls lived there, but I knew instinctively that none of
them had taken it. I went straight to a room used only by
one of the maids. Going to a dusty cupboard, I knelt
down, reached to the back, and pulled out a shoe. In the
toe of it was my watch."

Surely she could be satisfied with such a happy ending.

The annals of parapsychology are full of experiences
similar to those of Mrs. Phillips, where people have tried
to suppress their sensitivity. Yet, when psychic talents
have been allowed to express themselves fully, on occasion the most startling information has been received.
This occurred in the case of a clairvoyant named Titus. A
detailed account of her experience was first published by
William James, the famous American psychologist who
was also a very active member of the psychical research
societies, and a strong defender of extrasensory perception. Here is Mrs. Titus's story in brief:

On Monday, October 31, 1898 Miss Bertha Huse left her
home in Enfield, New Hampshire before the rest of her family
was up. She was seen by several people walking toward the
Shaker Bridge over Lake Mascoma, and one person passed her
on the bridge. When she didn't return home later in the day
her family and friends began to search for her; and soon most
of the village had joined in the hunt. By evening a diver was

sent for from Boston. He arrived early Tuesday and searched the lake bottom for Bertha all that day and until noon on Wednesday without success.

On Wednesday night Mrs. George N. Titus of the nearby village of Lebanon, New Hampshire, dreamed that Bertha Huse had been drowned in the lake; and when she awoke she told her husband the exact position where the girl would be found. Mrs. Titus was known as a "clairvoyant." She never took money for the psychic information she produced, but her husband knew from experience that she most likely would be right about Bertha.

Her neighbors also were curious when they heard of her dream, and great crowds assembled at the Shaker Bridge when she appeared to tell the diver, Michael J. Sullivan, where to find the body. He resisted. "I searched there yesterday," he told her.

"You searched *there*," she said, "and *there* (pointing to certain spots), but you did not search *there*, and if you go down you will find her lodged in the timberwork under the bridge at just this spot. You will see only her rubber boot projecting from the timberwork."

To satisfy her, Sullivan put on his diving suit and went down at the place she indicated. After a few moments Bertha Huse's bonnet floated to the surface; and soon the diver came up with her body. Sullivan then admitted that he had not looked at that exact spot the day before because the brush and debris under the bridge were so thick there he couldn't see at all. He stated that he wouldn't have found the body even then, had it not been for the rubber boot projecting from the timberwork, just as Mrs. Titus had said.

Mr. Sullivan also declared that he was more afraid of the woman on the bridge than the body under it.

Extrasensory perception is a talent like music or art, which can be improved with practice. Thus, one who gives indications of a mild ESP can develop it to the point where he is able to receive highly evidential material. Such an individual was a young English girl of the latter part of the last century who is known in psychical literature as "Miss A.," although she was later identified as one Kate Wingfield. We have her own account of how she first learned that she had an aptitude for crystal-gazing—seeing pictures while looking into a reflecting surface.

Who Has ESP?

I happened one day to be lunching with some friends w
talked on' the subject [of crystal-gazing] and said that th
believed that a glass of clear water acted in the same mann
[as a crystal]. Two or three of us looked in glasses of wate
and after a little while I seemed to see at the bottom of m
glass a small gold key. This was so distinct that I looked
the tablecloth, thinking that there must be a real key the
There was none, and nothing to explain what I saw.

We bought a glass ball, and I gradually began to see a go
deal in it. I have since seen in several crystals, and in a moo
stone in a bracelet. It does not seem to matter much what t
smooth surface is; but I have sometimes fancied that the scen
were brighter if seen in a real crystal. Occasionally I s
things in a mirror, or even without any clear surface, as thoug
I were in the midst of them . . . I am in a perfectly norm
condition when I look; not sleepy, nor in a trance, nor unco
scious of my surroundings.

Miss A. developed her crystal-gazing to the poi
where she was able to see in the little quartz ball scene
of an informative nature. Sir Joseph Barnby, designate
as a well-known musician of the time, wrote in Novem
ber 1892* about his experiences with Miss A's crysta
gazing. He tells of several incidents in which he observe
her at work with her crystal ball while they were gues
at Longford, the home of Lord and Lady Radnor. H
concluded:

One more incident in connection with the extraordinar
powers of this young lady remains to be noted. While looking
her crystal during one of the days I spent at Longford, sh
described . . . a room which appeared to her to be a bedroom . .
She added, "There is a lady in the room, drying her hands on
towel." She pictured the lady as tall, dark, slightly foreign i
appearance with rather "an air" about her. This described wit
such astonishing accuracy my wife, and the room she was the
occupying at a hotel at Eastbourne, that I was impressed
ask for particulars as to dress, etc. She stated that the dre
was of serge, with a good deal of braid on the bodice and
strip of braid down one side of the skirt. This threw me off th
scent, as before I had started for Longford my wife had e
pressed regret that she had not a serge dress with her. M

*Proceedings S.P.R., vol. viii. pp 499-515.

astonishment, therefore, was great on returning to Eastbourne to find my wife wearing a serge dress exactly answering the description given above.

The sequel to this incident comes some sixteen months later on, when my wife and I attended a [theatrical] performance. We arrived early, and after placing my wife in a seat I moved about the room speaking to friends here and there. In the course of ten minutes or so, Lady Radnor and Miss A. entered the room. During the greetings which ensued, Miss A. called my attention to a standing figure, saying: "You will remember my seeing a lady in her bedroom while looking in my crystal; *that* is the lady I saw." *It was my wife!* I need only add that she had never seen my wife.

That was no lady, it was Sir Joseph Barnby's wife. And Miss A. knew her from a picture in a crystal ball. When such a person as the amiable and talented Miss A. develops or is naturally endowed with extrasensory perception to a high degree, he or she is usually thought of as a medium. People who do not know too much about psychical research are disposed to assume that all mediums are arbitrarily frauds, but this is not so. It is the charlatans who gain publicity. There have been a number of mediums of strong moral character about whom there has never been a word of criticism or suspicion. Among the better known of this reputation are Mrs. Eileen J. Garrett, one of our great modern mediums, who is president of the Parapsychology Foundation in New York City; Mrs. Gladys Osborne Leonard of Tankerton, Kent, England, now in her 80's; and Mrs. Leonore Piper of Boston, Massachusetts, who lived in the early part of the 20th Century. All these women have devoted their lives to helping science try to understand their strange psychic powers and to discover what causes them.

Despite the traditional acceptance of the Emerald Isle as the fatherland of supernormal beings, human and otherwise, ESP does not seem to be confined to specific geographical locations nor the inhabitants thereof. Of course, with such a big world and such a new science,

no systematic study of the distribution of psi capacity ove
the human race as a whole has yet been undertaker
Such a survey based on proper sampling may be long i
coming; and so any judgment made now will have t
depend upon only incidental samplings and the resul
taken for what they are worth. But from these sampling
we find, according to Drs. J. B. Rhine and J. Gaithe
Pratt in *Parapsychology Frontier Science of the Mina*
"much the same type of spontaneous experience widel
scattered, not only back through history to ancient time:
but over widely distinct ethnic groups as well."

In fact, the evidences of the possession of strong tele
pathic and clairvoyant powers by the aborigines of Dow
Under are most impressive. Rumored over the years, th
powerful psi of the aborigines has been substantiated b
recent investigation.

"It is true," says Arthur Abarbanell,* "that using n
other agency than their minds, savage bushmen in Aus
tralia can accurately transmit thoughts, feelings and idea
to friends and relatives one hundred miles away. They hav
reconstructed crimes, identified and tracked down crimin
als, and located strayed cattle and lost valuables.

"The Australian aborigines are one of the most primi
tive peoples. They live deep in the bush under condition
like those of the Stone Age. Centuries of struggle fo
existence appear to have sharpened their faculties; thei
eyes can identify small objects at great distances, even i
fog; their ears accurately interpret sounds inaudible to civ
ilized man; their noses distinguish between small ani
mals and human beings they cannot see or hear." Bu
their psychic powers are even more highly develope
Dr. A. P. Elkin, an anthropologist of Sidney University
was jolted from his scientific detachment by some of hi
experiences with the natives. In each village they kne

*"Are Aborigines Psychic?" *Tomorrow* Magazine, Vol. 9, No. 4, Autumn, 1961.

of his impending visit far in advance of his arrival. They knew where he had been previously and what his mission was. Yet investigation proved that his coming had not been announced by messenger, smoke signals, drums or other physical agency. His hosts explained: "Thoughts, though invisible, can be sent flying through the air."

Dr. Elkin cites scores of instances in *Aboriginal Men of High Degree* of natives receiving telepathic messages from distant homes informing them that a father had died, a wife had given birth, a sister had been killed, etc. Checking the information, he discovered that in each case it was accurate.

Controlled extrasensory perception tests among the aborigines of northern New South Wales have yielded astonishing results. Conducted under the auspices of Sidney University by psychologist Lyndon Rose, the tests followed the pattern devised by Dr. Rhine. In one of the tests five dice, each of a different color, were used. A native tossed the dice from a box one at a time and concentrated on the color exposed. In a hut out of sight sat another native under constant supervision. His part of the experiment was to guess the colors in the order in which they turned up. An average of twenty percent correct guesses is par for the course. Australian bushmen consistently averaged better than fifty percent correct!

In another experiment a cigarette was put into a tightly sealed box. Three aborigines imported from the bush ten miles away were separately shown the box and asked to identify the contents. One said it was a cigarette; the other two identified it as "tobacco and paper."

Abarbanel says: "To make the test more difficult, a cigarette holder was sealed in the box. Ten natives selected at random were admitted separately, shown the box, and challenged to guess its contents. None of them had ever seen a cigarette holder, or even heard of it.

Yet nine precisely described the shape, length, and color of the unknown object! Let me add that when this same experiment was performed at Duke University, only one in ten students guessed correctly."

The various methods of clairvoyance and divination of the Kaffir of South Africa have been investigated and confirmed by numerous authorities, Abarbanel goes on. "Despite restrictions and a decline in the number of recognized native witch doctors, there are still quite a few of them whose psychic powers are remarkable. These Kaffir 'doctors' are not chosen at random. The tribal chiefs must be convinced of their psychic gifts before they are permitted to develop them. Only when the training diviner is satisfied with his apprentice's susceptibility to psychic influence, will he be initiated into the secrets and customs known only to witch doctors."

Even primitive peoples do not show extrasensory perception as strongly as animals do. Confronted with uncharted animal behavior, a perplexed zoologist or naturalist will sometimes turn from the usual consideration of mechanistic function and suggest traits of ESP. And parapsychologists are inclined to accept the possibility. Among the familiar animal feats that still remain a puzzle are the long migratory travels of certain species —the eel hatched near Bermuda which finds its way across the Atlantic into the Mediterranean and then up the rivers of Europe to the very place where its ancestors lived; the salmon who faithfully goes back upstream every year to the same fresh water spot to spawn. For all the talk of "built-in radar" and "gyroscopic compass," we don't really know how homing pigeons go home. These phenomena have not been officially attributed to extrasensory perception; but there is a reasonable likelihood that it is the answer.

More convincing to many students is the ability of domestic animals to find their way back over long distances, sometimes after having been removed from the original location in closed vehicles and by an indirect route. Even more baffling are those human interest accounts of pet cats and dogs left behind or lost when the owners move to a new home. Weeks, months, even a year later these pets, battered and footsore but grimly determined, arrive at the new home—a place they have never seen before, sometimes hundreds of miles from their former environment.

Such an animal was Old Tom, a member of the Coleman Feldman family which moved seventy-five miles from a Yucalpa, California ranch to Hollywood on April 14, 1961, leaving him behind. One year later the black cat appeared at the Feldman's Hollywood address. The new owners of the ranch said Old Tom vanished during the summer of 1961. The Feldmans identified him by the scars of his previous battles, and the family dog Candy, who has no use for strange cats, greeted his former pal with great affection.

4   *The History of ESP*

of paranormal manifestations are voluminous, and although the subjection of such phenomena to scientific investigation is comparatively recent, there was actually one "scientific" test made for ESP in the days of Ancient Greece.

Herodotus, the Father of History, tells about a king who may well have been the world's first psychical researcher. Alarmed at the growing power of the Persians, Croesus, King of Lydia from 560 to 546 B.C., decided to consult an oracle as to what he should do. But he wanted his help to come from the one who seemed the most gifted. Accordingly he chose seven oracles (six Greek and one Egyptian) and sent out seven messengers with the instructions that on the hundredth day after their departure each should ask his oracle, "What is King Croesus, the son of Alyattes, doing now?" The messengers dutifully wrote down the answers and brought them back to Croesus. Five of the oracles flunked the test. The sixth was warm. But before the question was even put to the seventh, the famous oracle of Delphi, she recited a verse to the messenger.

> . . . Lo, on my sense there striketh the smell of a shell-covered tortoise,
>> Boiling now on a fire, with the flesh of a lamb in a cauldron—
>> Brass is the vessel below, and brass the cover above it.

And what *was* the king doing that day? He was whipping up a lamb and tortoise ragout in a brass cauldron, covered over with a lid which was also of brass.

Socrates, philosopher, teacher, and intimate friend and counselor of the great men of his day, was constantly observed by Plato, who recorded his life as devotedly in detail as ever Boswell did Samuel Johnson's. From Plato we learn that Socrates had amazing physical health and endurance as well as a brilliant mind. He could drink deeper, talk longer, and walk farther than any man of his time, and what he said always indicated great sanity and shrewdness. Socrates regularly informed his associates that he was guided in all his affairs by an inner monitory voice which he called his "daemon." This word is not to be interpreted as "demon," but signified either a god or goddess, or the soul of a living man, or the spirit of a dead one. In what exact sense Socrates himself defined the word we do not know for sure. But it was a voice of restraint, with an uncanny sagacity on which Socrates invariably relied.

If on all occasions this inner voice had produced what it did most of the time—such counsel as might have originated from Socrates' own wiser self—then we could think of his daemon as his conscience. But this is not the way it operated. On several recorded occasions it gave him knowledge which can be listed as extrasensory.

Plutarch tells how when walking and discoursing with friends, Socrates stopped suddenly and listened to his daemon, then told them all to turn back and go by another street. Most of his companions followed him on the detour, but others kept on their way as planned, and presently met a great herd of swine which knocked down some of them and fouled the rest.

In the Platonic dialogue *Theages,* the story of Timarchus is related. There was a secret plot to assassinate this man, and Socrates' daemon seemed to know of it, although the rest of the gathering at which Socrates and Timarchus were present did not. When Timarchus started to leave, he was stopped by Socrates. "By no means rise from the table, for the accustomed warning has come to me," he said. Timarchus tried to go several times again, and was always warned by Socrates to stay. But then he apparently decided not to humor such foolishness, and he slipped out quietly when Socrates was not looking —to his doom.

The Bible is full of the very manifestations that psychical research is investigating today. Poet, playwright, and psychical student Louis K. Anspacher points out in *Challenge of the Unknown** that these have been interwoven with much myth and Oriental exaggeration, they have been arabesqued with all manner of allegorical imagination. "But," he says, "if we look deeply enough for it, we can see that the true kernel of a psychic phenomenon is often present." The organized churches of today abjure us to walk through the labyrinth of Biblical legend by faith and not by scientific fact. But, says Anspacher, "The early Church utilized psychical facts as literal testimony and persuasion."

As far as Anspacher could determine, all the great Biblical prophets, in their revelations, spoke under the influence of a controlling voice. "Sometimes," he writes, "this voice is attributed directly to God; but even when it is not, it is attributed to God by indirection through the inspired control or familiar spirit. The point is that the Old Testament is full of literal, factual descriptions of psychic phenomena which we encounter today in psychical research, and which were literally believed in the days of the early churches and not condemned."

It is a matter of religious choice how we interpret the supernormal feats mentioned in the Bible, whether they were Divinely inspired, whether they were performed by highly mediumistic people with extrasensory perception, or whether they were just plain theatrical magic. We read,

*Hill & Wang, New York, 1947.

in any event, that wizards, soothsayers (who predicted the future), witches and the like were active participants in those ancient cultures.

Tales of premonitions have always been common, one historical instance being Caesar's wife's foreboding dream on the night preceding the Ides of March. Shakespeare, in *Julius Caesar*, borrowed this account from the Greek biographer Plutarch, who told it originally. Plutarch says that Caesar was so impressed by Calpurnia's state of mind, never knowing her to be so affected before, that he nearly yielded to her entreaties not to go to the Senate. Had he refrained, a lot of good literature would have been lost.

Further great literature might also have been denied us, according to Boccaccio's book about the life of Dante. After the death of the great author of *The Divine Comedy*, several concluding cantos of the *Paradiso* had not been found. Dante's sons searched everywhere. Finally, they undertook to write the necessary verses themselves. This brought prompt action from the deceased Dante, for one of his sons, Jacopo, had a dream which led to the abandonment of what Boccaccio calls "such presumptuous folly."

In the dream, Dante appeared as a spirit and Jacopo lost no time in asking about the cantos. His father then led Jacopo to Dante's old bedroom in another house. Touching one of the walls, Dante said, "What you have sought for so much is here."

Jacopo awoke at once and, with witnesses, hurried to the house where his father had resided at the time of his death. Fixed to the wall was a hanging which Jacopo may have seen but little noticed during his father's lifetime. Now he lifted it up and found a niche in the wall and in it the thirteen cantos needed to complete the *Commedia*. They were mouldy from dampness and would surely have crumbled away had they remained there much longer.

Belief in the supernatural was heavily emphasized in the Middle Ages, producing an abundance of saints on the one hand and of witches on the other. Perhaps saints and witches were merely hysterics, as many claim. And yet there seems, on the whole, to have been a certain amount of supernormal material produced by these persons which is difficult to account for entirely as hysteria. The reluctant though holy levitations of St. Mary Magdalen de'Pazzi and the prophetic mutterings of an entranced necromancer may well have sprung from the same innocent source.

It is true there were some who used their powers or their pretended powers for no good. But in many cases unfortunate individuals with suspected paranormal ability were caught up in the superstitious and bigoted air of their times and their peculiarities turned against them. Any departure from ordinary behavior patterns, anything unusual or eccentric in personality or even in physical appearance, branded the possessor as an instrument of the Devil. Not only the blind fear of ignorance, but jealousy, covetousness, revenge, spurned passion, or fanatic religious zeal, could readily turn a few precognitive dreams or mind-reading incidents into causes for accusation, and bring upon an unhappy soul with nothing more venal than a mild form of ESP undeserved, unjust, and terrible punishment.

Joan of Arc has been held to account by psychologists and historians for her "voices." But if she was mentally unstable or an hysteric, we should all be so afflicted. The advice her voices gave enabled her to command strange new situations with competence and genius. Her unhesitant selection of the unimpressive Charles VII from a group of courtiers persuaded him of her seriousness and her value to his cause. To the dedicated peasant girl, the very regal false king placed upon the throne to deceive her meant nothing. Charles may have been flattered, but he was also convinced of her powers. Her brief career was constantly directed by self-declared supernormal instruction, instances of which were duly set down to be used against her at her trial. She predicted that she would be wounded at Orleans, as she was, and at the height of her acclaim she said repeatedly that she would "last but one year or a little more." And she did.

Among the many accounts of the Maid that set her as one apart is the legend of how she got her sword. In the earth behind the altar of the Church of St. Catherine at Fierbois, a church she had never seen, her voices told her that a sword was buried. A man utterly unknown to her was sent for it. He dug behind the altar and found the sword exactly where she said it would be.

From the mid-16th century come the legacies of Nostradamus. Many of these strange prophecies are in such figurative language that their application to specific future events is notoriously inconclusive. But on occasion Nostradamus predicted with such directness that his meaning is startlingly clear. Such was his statement that: "The young lion will conquer the old one upon the field in single combat. He will pierce his eyes in a golden cage, who will then die a dreadful death." In July, 1559, King Henry II gave a tournament and entered the lists himself against the Earl of Montgomery, a young Scottish nobleman. As their lances broke on each other's shields, a splinter from the Earl's weapon went through the bars of the king's gilded helmet, pierced his eye, and brought an agonizing death.

In 1788 Jacques Cazotte, reputed in France to have a sixth sense, announced at a dinner party the course of the revolution impending, he said, for France, and told in detail the tragic fates awaiting various guests at the board. Some would take their own lives to cheat the executioner, but most would die by the guillotine. Cazotte even predicted his own death on the scaffold. A man named LaHarpe made notes of these predictions and they were widely circulated before the start of the revolution. According to reports, every word of them came true for every member of that dinner party.

Emmanuel Swedenborg predated radio and television by nearly two hundred years, yet he once gave an on-the-scene description of a fire in a distant city which equaled the efforts of any veteran newscaster with all the facilities of modern communication at his disposal. On a Saturday at 4 p.m. Swedenborg, who had just arrived in Gottenburg from England, became restless and left his friends, to walk about outside. When he returned he reported that a conflagration had just broken out near his home in Stockholm. It was spreading very fast, he declared with agitation. He continued to be upset until 8 o'clock, when he joyfully exclaimed, "Thank God! The fire is extinguished third door from my house."

His clairvoyance arousing great interest as word spread throughout the city of Gottenburg, Swedenborg was summoned before the Governor, for whom he described the fire precisely. It was not until the following Monday that a royal messenger arrived from Stockholm with word of the holocaust, confirming the minute accuracy of Swedenborg's account.

This and other stories about the great Swedish seer were investigated and written up by the distinguished German philosopher Immanuel Kant. They only added to Swedenborg's luster, for he was already eminent as a philosopher, mathematician, and scientist, who was made a Count by Queen Ulrica for his accomplishments. He originated a great religious system called Swedenborgianism, the tenets of which are largely incorporated in the Church of the New Jerusalem, founded some years after his death.

The early days of the 19th Century saw the introduction of mesmerism, developed by Franz Anton Mesmer from his theory of animal magnetism. Mesmer's reputation as a sincere man of science was a trifle cloudy and his demonstrations of mesmerism were regarded with considerable suspicion. Because it was at first believed that the mesmeric condition was a sleep-state, Dr. James Braid, an English surgeon, gave it the name of hypnotism. He was the first person really to take it seriously, despite the violent opposition of his colleagues; but it gradually became accepted by other people of integrity and for a little while enjoyed quite a vogue in the medical profession. Such physicians as Dr. James Esdaile and Dr. John Elliotson discovered its capacity to put people in a condition where they could undergo surgery without pain. But as ether and then other anaesthetics came into use, for almost a century hypnotism was relegated to show business, to compete as public entertainment with acrobats, comedians, and animal acts. Now it has been reinstated as a valuable agent in dentistry, surgery, psychiatry and childbirth.

During some of the early experiments with hypnotism a peculiar condition was discovered. An 1831 report states that a mesmerized subject was able to read with the eyes shut, even when the eyelids were held closed with the fingers. A commission investigating mesmerism between 1826 and 1831 reported that some persons in the trance state could make diagnoses and divine the nature of a malady as though they were actually seeing the individual organs of the sick person.

In 1840 the Reverend C. H. Townshend stated that if anyone struck him or hurt him in any part of his body while he had a certain young woman under hypnosis, she would appear to suffer pain in the corresponding area. Dr. Esdaile observed in India in 1846 that if any object were put into his mouth a Hindu boy he had hypnotized could recognize the taste of them. Dr. Elliotson reported similar experiences.

This thought transference being observed was believed to be a feature of hypnosis itself, and a number of studies were made on that assumption. Dr. E. Azam, a French physician, discovered that he could achieve effects similar to those reported by Esdaile and Elliotson. He found that if he put table salt into his mouth, one of his patients, when hypnotized, seemed to taste salt herself.

Tests were carried out by various hypnotists to confirm the transmission of the sensation of pain. If a pin was stuck into the left hand of the doctor, the subject would jump and rub his left hand. Experiments were made to determine whether the subject could identify accurately the spots on which the hypnotist had been pinched. Even when the two protagonists were in separate rooms and out of possible visual range, these tests were still successful. Then hypnotism at a distance was accomplished.

Dr. Pierre Janet of the Sorbonne was one of several French physicians who induced hypnotic trance in their subjects from distances great enough to rule out any possibility of physical communication. In twenty-five trials Dr. Janet succeeded in putting the subject into complete trance eighteen times. In four of the remaining trials the hypnosis was partial. Anticipating the disapproval of his conservative colleagues, Dr. Janet did not publish a report of his experiments.

The fact that extrasensory perception was associated with hypnosis at first was a fortunate error, Dr. Rhine believes, "because it advanced the problem of thought transference to the point of experimental study. By the time it was understood that the two phenomena were essentially different, telepathy had become a subject for research in its own right."

5 ESP Declares Itself

IT WAS IN 1875 THAT PROfessor William F. Barrett of the University of Dublin, later knighted for his eminent work in physics, brought to the attention of his associates his discovery that thought transference could exist independently of hypnotism. This was received with enthusiastic indifference.

In 1880 the Reverend A. M. Creery of Buxton, England, began some experiments in his home with thought transference. One or another of his daughters or a young maidservant, says the account in *Phantasms of the Living,** would be sent out of the room and then the others remaining would fix their thoughts on some certain object which the absent one was to name when returning. The Reverend Creery reports in his lambrequin-trimmed Victorian style:

> After a few trials the successes preponderated so much over the failures that we were all convinced there was something very wonderful coming under our notice. Night after night, for several months, we spent an hour or two each evening in varying conditions of the experiments, and choosing new subjects for thought transference.
>
> We began by selecting the simplest objects in the room; then chose names of towns, names of people, dates, cards out of a pack, lines from different poems, etc., in fact, anything or series of ideas that those present could keep steadily before their minds; and when the children were in good humor and excited by the wonderful nature of their successful guessing, they very seldom made a mistake. I have seen 17 cards, chosen by myself, named right in succession, without any mistake.
>
> We soon found that a great deal depended on the steadiness with which the ideas were kept before the minds of "the thinkers," and upon the energy with which they willed the ideas to

*By Edmund Gurney, Frederic W. H. Myers, and Frank Podmore. London, Trubner and Co., 1886.

pass. Our worst experiments before strangers have invariably been when the company was dull and undemonstrative; and we are all convinced that when mistakes are made, the fault rests, for the most part, with the thinkers rather than with the thought-readers.

During the next two years a large number of experiments were made with the Creery family, first by Professor Barrett, and then by members of the Society for Psychical Research. For by then there was an organization for the specific purpose of studying such material as that produced by the Creerys. A group of Cambridge men under the impetus of F.W.H. Myers, a poet and classical scholar, and Edmund Gurney, whose field was psychology, and with the enthusiastic support of Barrett, decided to organize to investigate, analyze, and give careful scientific attention to the various supernormal phenomena coming under their observation. Their first president, Cambridge Professor Henry Sidgwick, and his wife, Eleanor Mildred, a sister of Prime Minister Arthur J. Balfour, Earl of Balfour, carried on with the examination of the Creery family, and so did members of the S.P.R.'s Committee on Thought Transference. This committee later stated that it was to tests with the Creerys that they owed "our conviction of the possibility of genuine thought transference between persons in a normal state."

Illustrating the fleeting nature of this and other forms of abnormal sensitiveness, the faculty of telepathy (a name Myers had coined for thought transference) soon declined in the Creery children, which behavior is consistent with facts observed to the present day. According to Gurney, if a group of friends tried it at home, they succeeded "when the spectators were interested and the percipient excited and confident." However, a series of failures always occurred when good results were anxiously awaited. This, Gurney explains, is because the subject of the experiment, who has aroused interest by several creditable demonstrations, feels responsible for continued success; and any self-conscious preoccupation on his part with trying to be successful seems fatal to his performance.

It may be observed that all this experimentation was being made to determine the characteristics of psychic capacity as well as for evidence of its existence. Throughout all subsequent experimentation psi has remained so nebulous a trait, so elusive and unfathomable, that no exact explanation of its constitution has ever been formulated. Consequently, research has taken the direction of trying primarily to prove its existence. And tests have been made over and over again for almost a century with the object of identifying various forms of extrasensory perception and very little more. One wonders why it seems necessary to researchers to repeat this so endlessly, until it is realized that because of psi's very intangibility, proving its existence on acceptable scientific grounds becomes an enormous challenge.

The importance of tests which would utilize chance probabilities was remarked by Gurney: "Of course the first question for science is not whether the phenomena can be produced to order, but whether in a sufficient number of series the proportion of successes to failure is markedly above the probable result of chance." This basic statement has been repeated endlessly by others.

Although Gurney spoke so wisely of chance, it is Professor Charles Richet of France who gets credit for the initial use of the mathematics of chance in evaluating results of telepathy tests. And in 1885 Sir Oliver Lodge, another great physicist who interested himself in psychical research, proposed that conclusive evidence for telepathy might be produced by card-guessing in quantities. He worked out a mathematical formula for estimating the number of hits above those to be expected by chance.

After the introduction of the mathematics of chance

and the use of playing cards, the tests for telepathy began to change from the old parlor-game technique. When the probability of naming the right card on the basis of chance was known it was easier to compute how much evidence of telepathy the results showed. While an experimenter in chemistry might be contented to achieve a result in which the odds were 20 to 1 against chance, in a subject as offbeat as psychical research it seemed imperative to devise a system in which results could be estimated which were 200, 2,000 or 20,000 to 1 against chance. With card tests repeated endlessly such results could be achieved.

The first tests performed in this manner are not now considered to have been as carefully and scientifically executed as are those which are currently conducted; yet many were surprisingly well done. The ideal way of testing for ESP has still not been devised.

As papers were published on the subject of telepathy in the *Proceedings* and *Journal* of the Society for Psychical Research, and as the techniques of card testing were explained, many read of them and became curious. People in England, America, France, Sweden, Poland, Germany, and Russia began to test themselves and their friends and to send in reports of their experiments to the S.P.R.

About 1885 Edmund Gurney collected seventeen groups of card-guessing experiments made by his friends. The total number of trials was 17,653. The number of successes exceeded mathematical expectation by an amount such that only twice in a hundred million times could these results be equalled by accident.

Gurney also reported 505 trials in which A. J. Shilton attempted to name which of four colors was being visualized by the sender. One-fourth right could have been produced by chance, but Shilton was able to name more than half correctly. The probability of this happening according to chance was trillions to one.

Gurney mentions further the experiments of the Misses Wingfield in calling numbers. Out of 2,624 trials, where the most probable number of successes was 29, the actual number obtained was 275. This result exceeded mere accident by a ratio of more than the ninth power of a trillion to one: visually, $1,000,000,000,000^9$ to 1.

Some experimenters began to use other methods of testing for telepathy. In some studies the sender (or agent or experimenter) would make a drawing and fix his attention upon it, while the receiver (or subject or percipient) would attempt to reproduce the drawing as accurately as he could. Comparison of the pictures gave the results in what has been called a qualitative manner.

Ever since these earliest experiments, the S.P.R. has been active in the examination of data and devices to prove or disprove the existence of supernormal powers. Although for many years telepathy received most of the attention, clairvoyance had also been revealed to experimenters when mesmerism was first looked into. In the beginning, the interest in thought transference overshadowed that in clairvoyance and research in this field was relatively meager. Though occasional tests for clairvoyance were made they were not considered important at that time.

As the S.P.R. matured and confidence increased, the Society investigators turned to other paranormal manifestations which were even more dramatic. It so happened that the late years of the 19th and those of the early 20th Centuries produced some of the most outstanding mediums of all time and these were available for study and observation. The S.P.R. made the most of the opportunity to give them its earnest consideration. The activities of the Society, and of the American Society for Psychical Research, which had been formed in 1885, now extended over a wide range of paranormal phenomena including house haunting, crystal gazing, table tipping, dowsing, fire walking, faith healing, and spirit photography; a truly formidable list.

The approach of these investigators was extremely careful and highly critical, with all demonstrations controlled as far as was humanly possible. Serious psychical researchers have always been extra careful in order not to be considered as far out as the matters with which they deal. Scientists in other fields have been vigorously disinclined to admit there was anything worth their time in haunted houses and ghosts, the maunderings of mediums, or the pranks of poltergeists. Tricks, folklore, hysteria, hallucination were the ready explanation of those unfamiliar with the data. Now, however, they have gradually become aware that there is more to extrasensory perception than can be casually shrugged off. Those with open minds, who have conscientiously read the published material dealing with experimental ESP, are now willing to admit not only its possibility but its actuality. They were very slow in coming to this viewpoint. But then, departures from tradition are seldom welcomed.

William Barrett attempted to bring some of his experimental work before the British Association for the Advancement of Science as early as 1871. His paper was met with ridicule and the Association refused to publish it.

When, around 1915, Dr. John E. Coover of Stanford University tested his psychology students and others and obtained evidence of telepathic ability, he declined to recognize his own findings. Even when their significance was repeatedly pointed out to him by those who checked and re-evaluated his data, he preferred to believe that he had failed to find any evidence, and remained silent when corrected. For this reason he is often quoted as having "disproved" the existence of ESP.

Because of the loss of life in the First World War, the

Nineteen-twenties saw a marked rise in telepathy, and also, more particularly, in Spiritualism. Men and women felt the need of something more than purely physical explanations of life and death. During this time a mass telepathy experiment was conducted by radio over the Zenith Broadcasting Station in Chicago in 1923, and a little later the British Broadcasting Corporation conducted another. Later still, *The Scientific American* carried out a self-testing program in telepathy, and there were numerous other indications of popular interest.

There were two important university experiments in telepathy during the Twenties. Both of them were done in psychology laboratories, one in America and the other in Europe. Both were carried out by young psychologists, supported by the approval of older, more eminent men, and both introduced new procedures. At the University of Groningen in Holland, Dr. J. F. J. W. Brugmans, under the sponsorship of Professor G. Heymans, produced a test that was quite original and very successful. The best percipient was a young dentist, who was put, blindfolded, inside a tent-like enclosure of black curtains. In front of this tent was a board marked out in forty-eight squares, with a raised series of eight letters across the top and six figures along one side. By reaching out from the tent with his hands and feeling his way across the board from a letter and a figure, the dentist located a particular square. The experimenter sat in a room above him looking down through a hole in the floor directly over the board, so that he could see the subject's hands but could not be seen himself. The hole was covered with two layers of plate glass with an air space between them. From two bags, one containing letters, the other figures, the experimenter drew one letter and one figure at a time, and concentrated on the square they indicated.

The results were high enough to be dramatic. Out of 187 trials, where if chance had been operating the most probable number of hits would have been 4, the dentist picked the proper square 60 times. This, according to psychical researcher Rosalind Heywood,* was no less astronomical than if red had turned up at roulette 150 times running. "There is no mathematical certainty that such a thing cannot happen," she says, "but it is safe to say that any mathematician would stake his life against it."

The American research was done at Harvard University by Dr. G. H. Estabrooks, working under Professor William McDougall, who had recently transferred there from Oxford University. Estabrooks shuffled a pack of playing cards and looked at the top card, then signaled by means of an electric light that he was ready. The subject, who was in another room with two closed doors between, tried to identify the card of which Estabrooks was thinking. Twenty cards were tried at a sitting. After putting 83 subjects, who were Harvard students, through this test Estabrooks computed his total score and found the odds were a million to one against the result being due to chance.

Noticing the odd manner in which the proportion of hits declined toward the end of tests, Miss Ina Jephson of the S.P.R. conducted another significant card-naming experiment in 1928. When the hits suddenly fell disproportionately below the misses, Miss Jephson speculated that this might be the result of sheer boredom with the endless repetition. ESP was now functioning, as it were, in reverse. In Mrs. Heywood's words, "It does at least indicate that something other than chance is at work, particularly when at the end of an experiment the number of correct hits passes below the level of chance probability, for this suggests that percipients are unconsciously using ESP to express their boredom."

But aside from the comparatively few striking tests

*Beyond the Reach of Sense, New York, E. P. Dutton & Co. Inc., 1961.

we have mentioned, and some qualitative experiments we will discuss later, most of the findings regarding telepathy during this period were completely negative. At Columbia University and the University of London experiments made no headway. The mass experiment carried out by the S.P.R. and the British Broadcasting Company met with no success. From 1927 to 1929 Dr. S. G. Soal made thousands of careful tests, but his results, too, seemed obstinately negative. A few other experiments by well-known psychologists gave mildly positive, though not dramatic results.

Most of the psychological profession was solidly against having anything to do with ESP. And one could hardly blame them, because parapsychology seemed to them at this point more an illegitimate waif than a science of respectable parentage.

This is the way things stood in 1930. Materialism had been successfully challenged, but the scientific world was not convinced. Then there came upon the scene of psychical research a man who has individually done more than anyone to change the scientific attitude toward parapsychology—Dr. Joseph Banks Rhine.

6   *ESP Goes into the Laboratory*

IN 1930, DR. J. B. Rhine introduced what Eric J. Dingwall calls his "American genius for mass production" to the prior sporadic efforts to determine the positive existence of extrasensory perception. And Rhine's drive was the added impetus which brought parapsychology out of the dubious and uncertain backwaters and into the main scientific stream.

Dr. Rhine had previously worked for many years with plant physiology and botany, in which he took three degrees at the University of Chicago. His wife, Louisa E. Rhine, was also a graduate in this field. When they encountered some impressive reports of paranormal events they became interested in psychical research. After a year in which they both studied psychology at Harvard under Professor William McDougall, they were more than ever taken with parapsychology, in which McDougall had a keen interest.

Dr. Gardner Murphy, Director of Research for the Menninger Foundation, and President of the American Society for Psychical Research, says in *The Challenge of Psychical Research** that Professor McDougall "was known to champion the reality of various ideas quite repugnant to mechanistic psychology, and to be favorable to the telepathy hypothesis. He and Rhine believed in one another from the beginning, and when McDougall was called to the chair of psychology at Duke University, Durham, North Carolina, the Rhines followed him there. Here, McDougall offered warm encouragement and made a professional opportunity in parapsychology available. From

*Harper & Bros., New York, 1961.

1930 to 1934 the Rhines carried forward pioneer experimental investigations in telepathy and clairvoyance and related problems. Many students served as laboratory subjects, and during the latter part of this period graduate students in the psychological department acted as assistants."

With what S. G. Soal and Frederick Bateman have called his "unquenchable enthusiasm allied to a dogged pertinacity,"* Dr. Rhine immediately set out to break down the persistent opposition to extrasensory perception. He knew that it was necessary to find a method of examining paranormal phenomena which paralleled the laboratory techniques of other scientific research. He also knew that in order to rule out the argument that ESP was nothing but pure chance or coincidence, he would have to repeat his experiments in even greater numbers, and that he would have to perform each test under such rigid control that there could be no question of sensory cues. Helped by advances in the science of statistics, Rhine was able to devise techniques which made a very large number of experiments possible. First acting as agent himself, Dr. Rhine found the students responding to his stimulating personality with cooperative enthusiasm. He soon had a few star performers who were able to produce outstanding ESP.

The tests were made with what were at first called the Zener cards (now usually referred to as ESP cards). In a pack of twenty-five playing-size cards there are five each of five different symbols: circle, square, cross, star, and wave. When the cards are run face down, by the mathematics of probability the subject would expect to guess one symbol correctly out of five trials. Running the entire twenty-five cards, the subject may be expected to average five chance hits. Repeatedly getting more than five hits is acceptable as an indication of extrasen-

*In *Modern Experiments in Telepathy*. New Haven, Yale University Press, 1954.

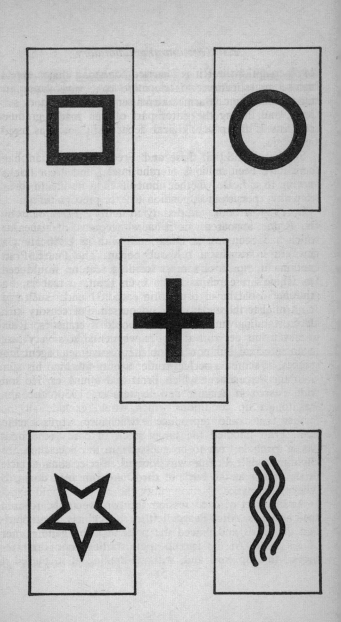

sory perception; but it is clearly understood that a single high-score performance is no more conclusive than putting a dime in a one-armed bandit and hitting the jackpot. Only when hundreds of runs have been made and the score is still higher than chance is the test to be considered significant.

Since the time that these cards were first used at Duke there have been millions of runs made, under conditions varying to indicate whether the ESP is to be identified as telepathy, clairvoyance, general ESP, or precognition.

In 1934 a book entitled *Extrasensory Perception* by Dr. Rhine appeared. In it were accounts of the tests which had been run at Duke; and with its publication a new era in psychical research began. The Pearce-Pratt experiment, the book's most startling feature, introduced Dr. Rhine's research assistant J. G. Pratt, at that time a graduate assistant in psychology, and Hubert E. Pearce Jr., a ministerial student since deceased. Pearce was such an outstanding subject that he would average from six to eleven hits per run at any experimental session. Once, in an informal but nonetheless impressive set of circumstances, he scored a perfect run of twenty-five hits.

In this experiment which Pratt and Rhine carried out with Pearce in August and September, 1933, the aim was to set up conditions which would exclude all the factors that could reproduce extrachance scores except ESP. Pratt handled the target pack of cards (the ones whose symbols were to be guessed) in the Social Science Building, while Pearce was located in a reading cubicle in the stacks at the back of the Duke Library 100 yards away.

At the start of each session the two men synchronized their watches. After Pearce left for his cubicle, Pratt shuffled the cards and placed the pack at a left-hand corner of his table. At the agreed-upon starting time Pratt removed the top card and, without looking at it, placed it face down on a book in the middle of the table and left it there for a minute. He then removed the card, still face down, to the right-hand corner of the table and immediately picked up the next card and put it on the book. This routine was continued until all the cards were transferred, one at a time, to the other corner. Thus twenty-five minutes were taken for each run of twenty-five trials. Pratt then looked at the faces of the cards and recorded in duplicate the order in which they had fallen and, as a safeguard, before he met with Pearce, sealed one copy in an envelope for delivery to Dr. Rhine.

In the meantime, Pearce had put down on his record sheet during each minute the symbol which he thought was on the card Pratt had in position at the time. At the end of the run he, too, made a duplicate of his record of the twenty-five calls and sealed one copy in an envelope for Rhine's records before checking his duplicate with Pratt. Thus each one of the men had individual records which they could check independently of the others. In this way, also, any question of the individual good faith of any one of the three was disposed of.

Two runs through the pack were made per day and the total series consisted of 12 runs or 300 trials. The number of hits expected on a theory of pure chance was 20% of 300 or 60 hits. Pearce obtained a total of 119 hits or just one short of double the number expected from chance. His average run score was 9.9 hits per 25 or 39.7% of the total trials made. A score as large as 119 hits in 300 trials would be expected to occur by chance only once in approximately a quadrillion (1,000,000,000,-000,000) of such experiments. The experimenters were sure, therefore, that every reasonable man would, without further argument, join them in dismissing the chance explanation. Their optimism was magnificent!

There are no known sensory processes that could be supposed to operate under these conditions. No type of rational inference could apply to a case of this kind. They, therefore, could hardly help but decide that, whatever clairvoyance or the extrasensory perception of objects *is,* this was a case of it. It was a case in which results were obtained under the strictest control ever until that time observed.

Such an experiment was a new and radical development in science, and, Dr. Rhine says, the report initiated "what was doubtless the most heated controversy American psychology has ever experienced." The results of the Pearce-Pratt experiment were attacked on the grounds of poor observation, mathematical inadequacy, and even fraud. It was suggested that all three experimenters had engaged in a colossal conspiracy to defraud. As to the latter, Dr. Hornell Hart of Florida Southern College says: "Such an hypothesis would disregard the immense probabilities of the reality of ESP which had been built up before these experiments, and the confirmations of the Duke results which have been established in the laboratories of various other universities."* But that didn't stop the critics.

Rhine's successes had an unexpected result, according to Rosalind Heywood. "The skeptics reversed their complaint, which had been that in previous experiments the odds against chance were too low to give evidence of the existence of ESP. They now said that in Rhine's experiments they were too high. Something must be wrong. There was a thunderstorm of criticism and every possible source of error was suggested."

But some of the criticism, or hypercriticism, while it might not have applied directly to the Pearce-Pratt experiments, could still be helpful in a general way to all ESP testing. So it was taken very seriously by Drs. Rhine and Pratt and their associates. They made efforts to cor-

*The Enigma of Survival, Charles C. Thomas, Springfield, Ill., 1959, p. 166.

rect anything to which these suggestions might intelligently apply.

For instance, the first Zener cards were accused of being too thin, and it was pointed out to Dr. Rhine that some persons might be able to read through their backs the symbols on their faces. Dr. Rhine immediately saw to it that new decks were made of thicker material.

Another criticism was that there was always a possibility that the sender, unknown to himself, might give certain unconscious cues which made the receiver's accurate guessing possible. It was suggested that involuntary whispering might occur which could be heard by the receiver, that when a sender concentrates on an object or mental image, he may whisper its name, or some associated word, under his breath. It was thought that he might unconsciously form the name of the symbol with his lips, or that his throat and mouth muscles might contract so that anyone familiar with muscle reading could know which was the key symbol. Though the sounds emitted by the agent might be far too faint for a guesser in the next room to be consciously aware of them, yet they might, it was suggested, be of sufficient intensity to register at a subconscious level.

The question is, of course, whether a person without moving his lips can produce either voluntary or involuntary whispers. If one attempts this himself, he will more than likely find that no listener can identify his sounds even when he speaks *aloud* without moving his lips. But the critics had still more of this type of detraction. They insisted that checks be made to see if the sender unconsciously reacted to a particular symbol by coughing, or tapping his feet. Tests proved that this was not the case.

The problem of inadequate shuffling of the cards was suggested—that during repeated shufflings by hand it might be possible for several cards to stick together. In research into card shuffling at Duke it was discovered that what came to be called a "psychic shuffle" could occur. ESP could be used to place the cards in the process of shuffling them so that they would match another pack of cards to a degree that ruled out chance as an explanation. After this surprising fact was learned, hand shuffling was discontinued altogether and shuffling machines were substituted. And then, even, special cuts were concocted to eliminate any possibility of interference from the mind of the subject. In many tests now performed a table of random numbers is used to prepare the deck so that each symbol is bound to be in a scientifically haphazard position.

There were accusations that errors in recording must account for the greater-than-chance results. To check the possibility of this, Dr. Gardner Murphy made numerous re-evaluations of previously scored tests. His check turned up about one error in 1,000 trials, slips which were incapable of invalidating the scoring. In addition, in one exhaustive recheck of 500,000 card matchings, only 90 mistakes were found. Seventy-six of these were target hits that had not been recorded. It is now accepted, from many rechecks of both successful and unsuccessful data, that in no case was error in checking sufficient to affect results significantly.

To counteract the assumption that his mathematics might be wrong, Dr. Rhine called in the American Institute of Mathematical Statistics for an appraisal of his conclusions. Their reply was: "On the statistical side recent mathematical work has established the fact that, assuming that the experiments have been properly performed, the statistical analysis is essentially valid. If the Rhine investigation is to be fairly attacked, it must be on other than mathematical grounds."

While spending years giving careful consideration to all the criticisms of their previous work, Drs. Rhine and Pratt were at the same time conducting numerous experiments to see if results above chance could still be obtained when safeguards were set up against all counter-hypotheses that had been suggested.

One of the most striking of these new tests was the Pratt-Woodruff series carried out in 1939. This experiment was designed to meet all the criticisms that had flourished during the years of controversy. "In the entire history of psychology," Dr. Rhine says, "no experiment has ever been carried out with such elaborate controls against all possible error."

Dr. Pratt and Dr. J. L. Woodruff, then a graduate student in psychology at Duke, designed a test for clairvoyance which was to control against both conscious and unconscious error. Dr. Pratt's function was to insure that all the precautions outlined were in full force throughout the test. The experimenter was Woodruff and the subjects were students.

Woodruff held a shuffled pack of ESP cards, the targets which were to be identified, face down behind an opaque screen. The subject on the opposite side of the screen had five key cards, on each of which was printed a different one of the five Zener symbols, hung up on his side of the screen so that Woodruff could not see their order, selected by the use of a random numbers book. In the operation of the test the subject pointed below the card on the screen which he thought matched the top card in the target pack which Woodruff held in his hand. At no time did Woodruff look at the cards during the test. At the end of each run Woodruff turned the cards over and recorded their position before learning the order of the key cards, and Pratt recorded the position of the key cards before knowing the order in which the target cards had been laid. Each man deposited a copy of his record in a locked box, and only then, after removing the screen, did they check the target cards against the five key cards. Dr. Rhine says: "Thus the location of the experimenters and the entire arrangement of the test were such that neither experimenter alone could willingly or unwittingly produce any sort of error that could bring about extra chance results. Neither could the subject. This research report was published and there has been no reasonable criticism made of this experiment and no call for a further improvement of its controls."

The results were that in 2,400 runs through the pack there were 489 hits above the number to be expected. The chance likelihood of this occurrence is again around one in a million. "The results, therefore," adds Rhine, "were not due to chance. No explanation has been proposed that will account for them except that of extrasensory perception."

Right after the publication of Rhine's book *Extrasensory Perception* in 1934, psychical researchers had all been exuberant. Dr. R. H. Thouless of the Psychology Department at Cambridge University commented: "His methods are so simple and his results are so clear, that his experiments can be easily repeated, and it will be possible without difficulty to convince ourselves whether Rhine's conclusions are valid or whether they are due to some flaw in his experimental methods."

But nothing happened. A new series of experiments in England designed exactly like Rhine's were unproductive of more than chance results. Between 1934 and 1939 Dr. S. G. Soal organized 160 persons to make 128,350 guesses with ESP cards. As a university lecturer he could do this work only in his spare time. He had to have forms printed and distributed, controlled conditions planned and all arrangements made, subjects found and instructed, reliable assistants secured to observe as guarantee against fraud. Then he had to set out on the monotonous, repetitive experiments themselves; and after they were over came the interminable labor of assessing the finished product.

And after all this, Dr. Soal's results were negative. It

was discouraging to all British parapsychologists. Why, if Rhine could succeed in the United States, could not others do so in England? The faith of some began to waver. Had Rhine really done it after all? Was there not perhaps some normal explanation for his results which had evaded them all? Experimental research in England had reached such a low point that even staunch enthusiasts of all psi endeavors had begun to question the success of their co-worker across the Atlantic.

7 ESP Returns to England

frustration was temporary. A new figure soon appeared in Britain who produced the same kind of well-founded results that distinguished Dr. Rhine. And his personality and techniques threw light on Rhine's accomplishments as well as his own. For G. N. M. Tyrrell possessed the same rare combination of qualities needed for dealing with so elusive a trait as ESP, hidden as it is in the subconscious. Tyrrell, a former radio engineer who had deserted electronics for psychical research, possessed not only scientific training but also a sympathetic approach which never impeded a subject who might be hesitant and doubtful of his extrasensory powers. In addition he had the ability to make a general conception from apparently unrelated particulars. After the report of Tyrrell's test was published, parapsychologists realized that it was also these qualities in Rhine that were largely responsible for his achievements.

Tyrrell was keenly aware, according to Rosalind Heywood, who knew him well, of a fact that "most researchers, intent on making their experimental conditions as like as possible to those of the physical sciences, had tended to forget. This was that physical conditions are not the only ones operative in ESP. Psychological conditions, he told his fellow experimenters with some emphasis, were equally important. The reason they were surprised at being unable to duplicate Rhine's successes was their own *a priori* conception of ESP. They assumed it to be a fixed characteristic possessed by A., but not by B., and one which could always be revealed by a simple test with a

pack of cards. But they were wrong. That so many percent of Dr. Rhine's subjects scored high did not imply
that the same percentage would do so anywhere, in any
conditions. The experimenter's task, said Tyrrell, is to
remove the percipient's inhibitions—to induce the faculty
to work—to get the extrasensory material externalized.
This needs personal influence."

Tyrrell was able to study at first hand the subtle influences which affect ESP, because his adopted daughter,
Miss Gertrude Johnson, was an unusually gifted sensitive.
Tyrrell and his wife created a calm and cheerful atmosphere in which her ESP could flourish unchecked, and he
tested her frequently. Miss Johnson is no temperamental
psychic, but is a sensible, practical and equable woman
and an unusually successful teacher of young children,
Mrs. Heywood tells us. She writes:

"Tyrrell was thus able to watch the rise and fall of the
ESP faculty in varying psychological conditions. It appeared to flicker, he said, like shadows in firelight. Friendly
positive encouragement would stimulate it, chilly and re-
pressive surroundings damp it out. The most subtle social
and personal influences made all the difference between
success and failure. He was the first to point out that to
repeat Rhine's experiments the equivalent of Rhine's
own influence must be included, and that the success of
certain methods in physics did not imply their success in
psychology. We cannot, he said, dictate to nature the
conditions under which we will accept results. We must
try and find out the conditions in which she will give them."

Tyrrell experimented at length with Miss Johnson
and then published his findings.* For his tests he devised
five little boxes, padded inside. These he placed in a row.
On top of the boxes, across the middle, he set an opaque
screen, concealing half of each box from its other half.
He was to sit on one side of the screen, Miss Johnson on

Science and Psychical Phenomena, Methuen, 1938.

the other. His half of the boxes were open, hers had light-proof lids. Tyrrell and Miss Johnson then proceeded to play not "who dunnit?" but "which izzit?" He would put the end of a wooden pointer silently into a box. Miss Johnson would instantly open the lid of her half of the box she thought he had chosen. In 30,000 trials, lasting five months, she approximated the same proportion of correct hits as were produced by Rhine's best performers, the odds being billions of billions to one.

Gertrude Johnson was tested by others besides Tyrrell, and the odds were still significant, though less spectacular. Tyrrell himself tested additional percipients and was highly successful, but the Tyrrell-Johnson combination far exceeded them all. These experiments were duly witnessed by eminent members of the S.P.R.

As usual, those who could not accept anything supernormal as the answer suggested every alternative to ESP. So Tyrrell set about elaborating and improving his apparatus in order to eliminate the human element entirely. The five boxes were retained, but instead of using a pointer, Tyrrell fitted each with a small electric bulb, which lighted up when he pressed the corresponding key; and the number of trials and successes was automatically recorded on a paper tape. This provided a completely objective record of the work, and obviated all risk of unwitting mis-scoring of hits. Significant results were still obtained.

Whately Carington in his book *Thought Transference** tells of the numerous refinements that were introduced from time to time into Tyrrell's procedures in answer to various criticisms and suggestions. The most interesting of all, Carington thinks, was the use of a "delayed action relay." This was so arranged that when the key was pressed, a bulb would not light until *after* the lid of the box was raised and then only if it was the correct lid, de-

*New York, Creative Age Press, 1946.

termined by the apparatus beforehand. This brought an element of possible precognition into the tests, not, of course, on the part of the machine but of the percipient.

"I am not sure," Carington concludes, "that this is not the most rigorous test of its kind ever attempted." Unfortunately, Tyrrell's operations were temporarily suspended by the Second World War, a bomb in the attic seeming to have put an end to his testing apparatus. But by then Whately Carington himself was making psychical history with his own experiments.

Science had been Carington's first love while he was still at Eton, and later at Cambridge University. World War I interfered with his studies as he left to join the Royal Flying Corps. Eventually a disastrous forced landing permanently damaged his health and he gave up flying. After the war he returned to Cambridge for the Air Ministry and War Office to do research in acoustics with special reference to psychological problems. He published a book about his highly original methods of mathematical assessments, but then became interested in psychical research and gave up all other work to concentrate on statistical evaluations in this field.

Rosalind Heywood tells us that "By the end of the thirties Carington had grown tired of bare experiments of the card-guessing type which seemed to him able to demonstrate little more than the mere fact of ESP. So he devised a more revealing pattern. This was to combine the old qualitative experiments with drawings with statistical methods of assessment. His procedure was simple enough. At 7 p.m. on ten successive evenings he would hang up one of a series of ten drawings in his study. Each drawing depicted a single target object which had been chosen at random. They remained there with the door locked until 9:30 the next morning. Between those hours his percipients—he collected 251 of them, all living at a distance—had to draw what they imagined to be the target object on a form prepared by himself. This series of ten constituted one experiment. After a gap in time the procedure was repeated. When a group of experiments was over, the shuffled drawings from the whole group were sent to an outside judge for matching up with the shuffled originals.

"Carington did eleven experiments and collected 20,000 drawings. Such experiments sound fairly straight-forward to organize. In fact, the job is enormous. There is first the problem of choosing the objects." He knew that they must be chosen at random, and he chose a watertight method of doing this. He then opened a set of mathematical tables at random, having decided that, say, the fifth number in the sixth column of the page he happened upon would indicate the page in the dictionary on which he would find his target object. He then drew the first drawable word on that page. But assessment of hits was a far worse headache and involved an immense amount of labor. How much were percipients influenced by outside events, for instance? If the word *boat* came up as a target on the night of the Boat Race, how spurious would a correct hit upon it be? Again, was visual similarity a hit, or must the percipient interpret his image correctly? If the target, for instance, was a peach, drawn with a twig and two leaves, and the percipient drew a round fruit with a twig and two leaves but labelled it an orange, Carington was stern about it. He would not allow it to be called a hit. He was taking no chances of being criticized for being too lenient.

Heywood goes on: "Another snag in assessment—in a way this was the worst of all—was that if psi were not operating, percipients would clearly be more inclined to draw everyday objects, such as a house or a dog or a motorcar, than, say, a duck-billed platypus. In other words, every hit was not of the same value and some, of course, would just be lucky coincidences. Carington's solution here was to make a list of ten thousand objects which had been drawn by percipients in his earliest experiments and note how often each had been drawn, irrespective of targets. He then valued hits on targets in reverse order to their popularity in this list, giving the most points to the object which had been least often drawn and vice versa."

These experiments with drawings were a marked success, for the hits were significantly more than one would expect from chance. But in addition the experiments gave some clues about ESP which had not previously been suspected. Carington found, for instance, that percipients seemed to pick up ideas more often than visual forms, also that it did not seem to matter whether the target was actually drawn, so long as the agent had thought of it. But the most unexpected revelation was of the existence of "displacement."

Hits on a particular target were naturally most frequent on the night it was drawn. If the target on Monday was a pyramid, most percipients who drew pyramids drew them on Monday. But some people also drew pyramids on Sunday or Tuesday, even sometimes two days before or two days after Monday. This really started Carington to thinking. If hits on a target drawing could occur both before and after that drawing was made, what about card-naming experiments? Maybe similar displacement had occurred in them. Carington suggested this idea to Dr. Soal, who had made so many unsuccessful tests for ESP in previous years.

But Soal was thoroughly discouraged. He had little desire to sit down and analyze the 128,350 squares, crosses, waves, stars and circles of his biggest experiment all over again. Dr. Soal tells us* that: "With remarkable pertinacity Mr. Carington insisted that I should re-examine my experimental data. He suggested that I should com-

*Ibid.

pare each guess, not with the card for which it was originally intended, but with the immediately preceding and the immediately following card and count up the hits. For, according to Carington, the faculty of extrasensory cognition might not always succeed in hitting the object at which it was aimed. Just as a rifleman may show a personal bias which causes him persistently to strike the target at a point to the left or right of the bull's eye, so it might happen that the guesser at Zener cards all unwittingly was guessing correctly—not the card the experimenter was looking at—but a card which was one or two places earlier or later in the sequence . . . It was, however, in no very hopeful spirit that I began the task of searching my records for this displacement effect. And yet, within a few weeks, I had made two quite remarkable finds, which fully confirmed Carington's conjectures. From my records of the guesses of 160 persons I had discovered two whose results exhibited the kind of effect anticipated by Carington." A man named Basil Shackleton had been scoring on the card immediately after the target card; and Gloria Stewart had been scoring hits on either the card before or the one after.

Proportionately encouraged, Dr. Soal and Mrs. K. M. Goldney of the S.P.R. then set out on a new series of card-naming experiments with Basil Shackleton as the subject. They took even more extreme precautions than before, and they had remarkable success. ESP was enjoying a period of extremely healthy laboratory activity.

Interestingly enough, Dr. Soal seemed to get his best results in testing for telepathy. He had been surprised to learn that Dr. Rhine felt the evidence for telepathy to be much weaker than that for clairvoyance, for Soal considered his best subjects to have done very well in telepathy tests. Scoring no better than chance expectancy in clairvoyance experiments, Basil Shackleton proved extraordinarily able in those for telepathy, especially when precognition was involved. He struck the plus-1 card (the one immediately following the target card) 1,101 times in 3,789 trials, which represents odds against chance of 10^{35} to 1.

Gloria Stewart also ran up nothing unusual in clairvoyance, but her results with telepathy were quite another story. In a grand total of 37,100 trials she hit the target card 9,410 times. Chance expectancy for this number of trials was 7,420 hits. Her results showed odds against chance in the neighborhood of 10^{70} to 1.

Dr. Soal, like Carington, became bored to death with the ESP cards. Abandoning the impassive Zener symbols, he substituted cards on which were vividly colored pictures of an elephant, a giraffe, a lion, a pelican, and a zebra. The more photogenic fauna were gratefully received by his subjects. For, in a long series of tests, the subject's interest declines and ESP declines with it. Then what is known as "psi missing" occurs. At some point along the seemingly interminable runs, the percipient will suddenly start hitting consistently lower than chance expectancy because he is utterly fatigued and bored. This is another indication that ESP exists, and is an unconscious power; for if he consciously tried to miss he couldn't succeed at it any more than he could make successful hits by consciously trying to.

Other characteristics of ESP were established by laboratory experiments. Time and space were found to affect psi in no way. In the Pearce-Pratt tests, the two protagonists were 100 yards apart. Further tests were performed in England with subjects as distant as Scotland, Holland and the United States, and in the U.S. with subjects even in India; and the far away guessers did as well as those near at hand. Illness was no obstacle to extrasensory perception. Though mental states affected it, physical conditions apparently did not.

In parapsychology laboratories efforts have been made

to discover what it is in people that determines the kind of ESP experience they can have or whether they will have few, many or none. Dr. Louisa E. Rhine says:*

"This question has concerned experimenters ever since research on ESP began to be convincing. It is still unanswered, but not for lack of experimental attempts to answer it, to pin down a specific personality type and link it with the ability to use ESP. At first it looked like a fairly simple problem and a research plan to solve it could have been stated simply: separate those who do from those who do not give evidence of ESP and then give personality tests to each and find out what their differences are. The simplicity of this idea, unfortunately, was deceptive. In the experiments which have been carried out, most of the major ready-made psychological measures have been used repeatedly to see whether they would separate those with high ESP test scores from those who fail to score above chance expectation. The result has not been a neat separation, although some differences have been found.

"One of the most pronounced of these differences, small though it is, is connected with the familiar psychological distinction of introversion and extroversion. In a very general way, and subject to too many qualifications to go into here, the more sociable extroverts scored somewhat higher than their more reserved and less expressive brothers, the introverts. The margin of difference, however, was small and was far from being so definite that one could safely predict the results if he gave an ESP test to two friends, one more extroverted than the other."

Another point of interest is that those who believe in extrasensory perception get higher scores than those who do not, an inference one could readily accept without putting the hypothesis on trial. But on trial it has been put.

Ibid. p. 192.

A study of personality in relation to psi capacities has proved this, according to Dr. Gertrude Schmeidler, a psychologist at City College, New York. She found that when she gave ESP tests to her students in the classroom after first getting records of their attitudes toward the possibility of ESP (favorable and unfavorable) she could predict which would be successful. She called the favorable subjects "sheep" and the unfavorable "goats" and over almost two decades she has accumulated a vast amount of data in which this relationship held to a remarkable degree.

Despite all the brilliant if sporadic achievements of the laboratory in demonstrating extrasensory perception by quantitative experiments; in spite of the triumphs and incontrovertible mathematical proof; in spite of exhaustive and successful efforts by dedicated workers, the returns have been all too meager. The rational words of J. Fraser Nicol and his wife Betty H. Nicol must be taken into account. "The level of success," say* the Nicols, "in literally millions of experimental card tests is either nonexistent or so low as to bear little affinity with those psi manifestations of mediumship and spontaneous cases upon which this field was founded. Even with the *best* of experimental subjects, well over ninety per cent of the trials are a sheer waste of time. And with regard to the general run of experiments, it is safe to say that something like ninety-five per cent of them end up with a grim affirmation of the null hypothesis."

Accordingly, at the present time the trend of formal experimentation is away from quantitative testing and back toward the qualitative tests favored in the early days of this century, but with improved procedures and techniques. Nevertheless, it can be truthfully said that for all

*"Experimental Uses of Chemical Compounds," *Proceedings of Two Conferences on Parapsychology and Pharmacology*, Parapsychology Foundation, Inc., New York, 1961.

its shortcomings, quantitative testing served its purpose well and thoroughly in establishing investigation of the paranormal as a legitimate scientific pursuit.

8 *Qualitative ESP Testing*

I THINK OF A HAT AND concentrate my mind on it so intently that you, in another room trying to capture my thought, draw a picture of a hat. This is a qualitative experiment for ESP, and some of the best evidence for the existence of telepathy has been produced in just this manner.

Qualitative experiments, based on the degree of success of individual efforts, are happily different from the quantitative testing we have been discussing. Statistical quantitative conclusions are reached by the assembling of overwhelmingly repetitious numerical data, a highly boring procedure, to say the least. Qualitative testing, on the other hand, is considerably more engaging.

Qualitative results can also be controlled and evaluated statistically, as demonstrated by Whately Carington. Perhaps the first controlled experiments were attempted by Malcolm Guthrie in Liverpool, England in 1883. Guthrie, head of a large firm with many hundreds of employees, happened upon an article on thought transference in a magazine. As a sound British gentleman of commerce, he considered the idea all twaddle and bosh, and so expressed himself to a relative of his over the port and Stilton. This relative, who worked for Mr. Guthrie, then informed him that now that he had mentioned it, some of his own employees had been playing around with the idea. A group of his girls met frequently and attempted to transmit from mind to mind colors, geometrical figures, cards, and visible objects of all sorts.

To the horrified boss, this sounded like a new and insidious form of goofing off. He promptly let it be known that any thought transference during business hours would be severely frowned upon. However, his anonymous relative assured Mr. Guthrie that the girls were doing it on their own time, confining their activities to evening meetings, and were doing remarkably well.

Now Guthrie hadn't achieved his status as head of a large firm by having an entirely closed mind. Visiting one of the thought transference sessions, he observed certain things which impressed him greatly. So he took the little group under his wing, put his executive abilities to work, and set up rules of procedure. Wanting each meeting carefully reported so that there would be no mere heresay of the successes achieved, he arranged with his friend, James Birchall, honorable secretary of the Liverpool Literary and Philosophical Society, to make a full and complete record of every experiment.

In the months of October and November, 1883, about 150 sessions took place under test conditions. The girl who attempted the guesses was either sent out of the room entirely, or placed, blindfolded, in a distant corner of the room wherein the target picture was being drawn. A Miss Relph and a Miss Edwards proved to be the most sensitive of the group, and some of their achievements may be seen on the accompanying page.

In order to make the activities properly authentic, Mr. Guthrie then appealed to science students in Liverpool to take a hand and bring in their laboratory techniques. Among those who accepted his invitation was a young physicist who later became the famous Sir Oliver Lodge.

Even with the scientists' restrictions, results still continued unexpected and startling. Miss Edwards and Miss Relph went on reproducing approximately what was drawn. People were amazed. It *must* be fraud. But could either Guthrie or Birchall, men of distinction and of unassailable integrity, be accused of fraud? Furthermore, young Lodge controlled the experiments with the same

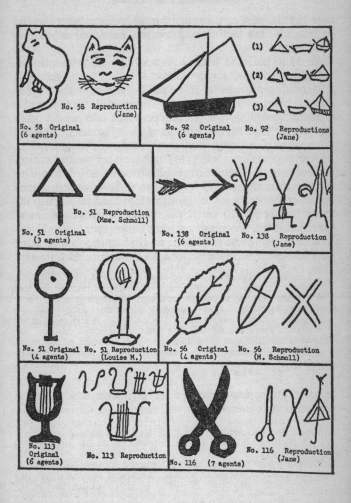

No. 58 Reproduction
(Jane)

No. 58 Original
(6 agents)

No. 92 Original
(6 agents)

No. 92 Reproductions
(Jane)

No. 51 Reproduction
(Mme. Schmoll)

No. 51 Original
(3 agents)

No. 138 Original
(6 agents)

No. 138 Reproduction
(Jane)

No. 51 Original No. 51 Reproduction
(4 agents) (Louise M.)

No. 56 Original No. 56 Reproduction
(4 agents) (M. Schmoll)

No. 113
Original
(6 agents)

No. 113 Reproduction

No. 116 (7 agents)

No. 116 Reproduction
(Jane)

care that he observed in his own laboratory. Accordingly, to this day, the Guthrie experiments have had a puzzling fascination.

In 1886 and 1887, Herr Anton Schmoll, with his wife and some friends, attempted two series of experiments in transmitting pictures by ESP, using the theory that a battery of senders should be more powerful than a single sender. Accordingly, in each experiment one person acted as receiver with four to nine as senders, concentrating upon a copy of a single, previously prepared, diagram. The opposite page shows what striking successes were obtained.

Professor Gilbert Murray of Oxford carried out with his daughter Rosalind, Mrs. Arnold Toynbee, two long series of experiments in thought transference during the years between 1910 and 1924. While Murray was out of the room Mrs. Toynbee, or some other agent, would announce to the persons present what she proposed to think of. Professor Murray describes the procedure as follows:*

> I go out of the room and of course out of earshot. Someone in the room, generally my eldest daughter, thinks of a scene or an incident or anything she likes, and says it aloud. It is written down, and I am called. I come in, usually take my daughter's hand, and then, if I have luck, describe in detail what she has thought of. The least disturbance of our customary method, change of time or place, presence of strangers, controversy and especially noise, is apt to make things go wrong. I become myself somewhat oversensitive and irritable, though not, I believe, to a noticeable degree. . .

Here are a few examples from experiments made on one particular evening.

> Mrs. Toynbee, agent: I think of Helena Cornford and Tony [a small grandchild] grown up, walking beside the river at Cambridge.
> Professor Murray, when he has returned to the room: This is not a book. It's got a sort of Cambridge feel in it. It's the Cornfords somehow. No—it's a girl walking beside the

*Proceedings S.P.R., Vol. 29 and Vol. 34.

river, but it isn't Frances [Mrs. Cornford]. Oh! Is it baby
Cornford grown up? Ought I to know what she is doing?
Mrs. Toynbee: Who is she with?
Professor Murray: No, I don't get who she is with—No, I
should only be guessing. . . No, I should only think of another
baby grown up—Tony.

Miss Agnes Murray, agent: Terence [a nephew of Professor
Murray's] and Napoleon standing on a hill above the Marne
and watching the artillery down below.
Professor Murray: This is a war scene—I don't get the persons
clearly, but I think on the hill looking down on the artillery.
It is not Saumarez. They may be Oxford people. I get the
bursting of shells. I should think it was Terence and somebody else—I don't think I know the other person. I don't
think I know him. No, I can't get him.

Miss Agnes Murray, agent: I think of *Diana of the Crossways.*
Diana walking up the road in the rain, and crouching down
in front of the empty grate in the house.
Professor Murray: This is a book. Oh, it's Meredith. It's Diana
walking. I don't remember the scene properly. Diana walking
in the rain. I feel as if she was revisiting her house, but I
can't remember when it happens.

Mrs. Toynbee, agent: I think of Rupert [Brooke] meeting
Natascha in *War and Peace.* Running in a yellow dress—
running through a wood.
Professor Murray: Well, I thought when I came into the room
it was about Rupert. Yes, it's fantastic. He's meeting some-
body out of a book. He's meeting Natascha in *War and
Peace.* I don't know what he is saying, perhaps, "Will you
run away with me?"
Mrs. Toynbee: Can't you get the scene?
Professor Murray: I should say it was in a wood.
Mrs. Toynbee: Color of the dress?
Professor Murray: No, I can't get it.

After such startling demonstrations as these, naturally
there were the usual many suggestions as to how they
could have come about by orthodox means. The most
popular explanation was that Professor Murray had hyper-
aesthesia—abnormally acute hearing. From the very start,
tests had been made to discover any auditory reinforce-

ment, but his hearing did not appear to be extraordinary or exceptional. Likewise, satisfactory precautions were taken to make sure that none of the conversation of the experimenters could be heard in the room to which Professor Murray retired. Witnesses further observed that even if his hearing were hyperacute, Murray's responses often gave information which had not been provided in the original announcement of the idea to be communicated:

Mrs. Toynbee, agent: *Greenmantle* [by John Buchan] where the German peasant woman takes them in in a snowstorm.

Professor Murray: This is something out of a book. I don't think I've read it. It's not Russian. It's got no particular national character. It's a snowstorm. It's somebody—I think it's a peasant woman giving shelter to a spy. I'm not sure. I think it's a German woman.

Mrs. Toynbee: What sort of a spy?

Professor Murray: I think he is English. I think it is a book of adventure.

The character in the book is a spy and an Englishman, but Mrs. Toynbee had neither mentioned this nor hinted of it in her original statement. Another thing which suggests telepathy rather than unusually sharp hearing is the way Professor Murray seemed to get his answers through a series of impressions:

Mr. Arnold Toynbee, agent: I'll do Rip Van Winkle coming down the mountain.

Professor Murray: Oh, I've got this. It's an old sort of gnome-like person with a matted beard coming down—very funny feeling expecting to be known and find things—Oh, it's Rip Van Winkle.

Or again:

Mr. Patrick Murray, agent: The lion in the Zoo trying to reach a large piece of meat just outside the cage.

Professor Murray: A sort of smell of wild animals—carnivorous animals. Something grabbing through bars at a piece of meat at a Zoo. Don't know the animal.

Stephen Murray, agent: George Hickey and me riding the motorbike past the inhabitants of Moulsford Lunatic Asylum, and one cheery-looking man with gold spectacles on his forehead barking furiously at us, like a dog.

Professor Murray: A curiously confused and ridiculous scene. You and someone on a motor bicycle, and a scene of great confusion—perhaps the bicycle is broken down. But there is a confused rabble and, I know it sounds ridiculous, but someone on all fours barking like a dog. (Then after a little encouragement) Are they lunatics by any chance?

The following is another instance where details are given by Murray which, while true, had not been mentioned.

Mrs. Toynbee, agent: I think of walking in the Park at Belgrade and meeting the English Governess.

Professor Murray: I'm getting a different feeling. It's somebody who is in rather a state of mind. I should think escaped from Russia. You are meeting her in some curious country. Wait a bit! It's not anyone at Robert College or Constantinople College. It's some queer country where you seem to be alone, and you are meeting some sort of Englishwoman who has been driven out of Russia, and hates the place where she is . . . Oh, yes, I do remember. It's when you went out to Constantinople by the express alone, and met the English governess in the Park.

Professor Murray says the history and state of mind of the English governess was correct, but had not been given. The "queer country" was Serbia.

Statistically the results of Murray's experiments were evaluated as follows: The first series, conducted between 1910 and 1915, comprised 505 experiments, of which 33% were judged successful, 28% partially successful and 39% failures. The second series of 295 experiments between 1916 and 1924 comprised 36% successes, 23% partial successes and 41% failures.

During the Nineteen-twenties several highly interesting researchs were carried out. René Warcollier, author of *Experiments in Telepathy,* science Professor Rudolf Tischner, German physician Dr. Carl Bruck, and the well-known American author of many best-selling novels, Upton Sinclair and his wife Mary Craig Sinclair, all contributed substantial evidence to the growing collection of testimonies for ESP.

After watching a young man's feats of apparent telepathy, Sinclair and his wife had become curious, although they were doubtful of the genuineness of the performance. Mrs. Sinclair decided to resolve her doubts by learning "to do these things myself." In the experiments she attempted, Mrs. Sinclair was the percipient, and her husband the agent. On occasion her brother-in-law, R. L. Irwin, who lived forty miles away, also acted as agent.

The experiments usually followed this uninvolved technique: The agent would make a set of drawings of fairly simple things—a bird's nest with eggs, a helmet, a tree, a flower—and enclose each one in its own opaque envelope. Then, or later, Mrs. Sinclair would relax on a couch, take the envelopes in hand one at a time, and after she considered that she knew its contents, she would draw them. She spent three years at it. Out of 290 drawings, 65 were judged successes, 155 partial successes, and 70 failures.

In his book *Mental Radio* Upton Sinclair said:

> For the past three years I have been watching this work, day by day and night by night, in our home. So at last I can say that I am no longer guessing . . . Regardless of what anybody can say, there will never again be a doubt in my mind. I KNOW!

Somewhat tempering the full-throated conviction of Sinclair, Professor William McDougall said of these tests that unless Mr. and Mrs. Sinclair were either grossly stupid, incompetent, and careless, or had deliberately entered upon a conspiracy to deceive the public, they had shown conclusive evidence of "some mode of communication not at present explicable in accepted scientific terms."

Volcano.

Black beetle.

Fish hook.

Flowers.

2 legs
of something
running

Alpine Hat.
TARGETS

Chafing Dish.
GUESSES

McDougall and Albert Einstein were both sufficiently impressed by the Sinclair results to appeal for a scientific hearing for *Mental Radio,* and both wrote introductions for the book.

The high degree of extrasensory perception displayed by Stephen Ossowiecki, a Polish engineer, inspired the Society for Psychical Research to conduct some rather extensive tests between London and Warsaw. Theodore Besterman, then Research Officer of the S.P.R., drew an ink bottle on ruled paper and near it wrote the words SWAN and INK. SWAN he underlined in blue and INK in red. He then put it into a series of three opaque envelopes. The envelopes were marked secretly so that tampering could be immediately recognized. They were next sealed in a special way with surgical tape. This packet was then sent to a group of psychical researchers in Warsaw and opened in the presence of Lord Charles Hope and two other members of the S.P.R. At that time Ossowiecki was allowed to handle the packet in the presence of the committee. (Psychic impressions are more frequently receivable when the object to be psychometrized—or read clairvoyantly—is held in the hand of the medium.) Sir Charles watched the envelope carefully while it was in the Polish engineer's grasp. Ossowiecki then proceeded to make drawings of what he thought had been enclosed, after which Lord Hope opened the three envelopes and compared Besterman's target drawings with Ossowiecki's. The first two of the medium's drawings were incomplete, but in the third he made only one mistake. He underlined the word SWAN in red instead of blue.

This test is reinforced by another carried out by anthropologist E. J. Dingwall, who wrote at the top of a sheet of paper the words: "Les vignobles du Rhin, de la Moselle et de la Bourgogne donnent un vin excellent." (The vineyards of the Rhine, the Moselle, and Burgundy produce an excellent wine.) On the lower half of the sheet he

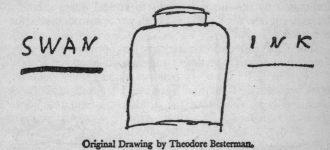

Original Drawing by Theodore Besterman.

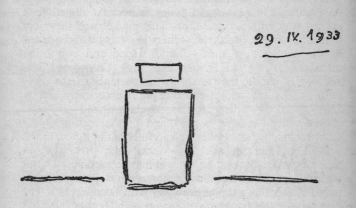

29. IV. 1933

Ossowiecki's First Attempt.

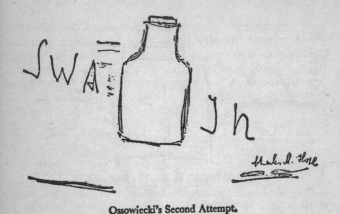

Ossowiecki's Second Attempt.

99. IX. 33

Ossowiecki's Third Attempt.

drew a very crude design meant to convey the idea of a bottle without actually being one. The folded sheet he then placed in an opaque red envelope. This he put into an opaque black envelope and the black envelope into a brown paper one, which he sealed. Then he pricked holes through the envelopes.

This packet was given to Ossowiecki together with two other white envelopes, in the presence of Dr. von Schrenck-Notzing and other trained observers. Some of the comments he made on Dr. Dingwall's envelope were as follows:

> I do not know why I see a little bottle. . . There is a drawing made by a man who is not an artist . . . something red with this bottle. . . There is without doubt a second red envelope. . . There is a square drawn at the corner of the paper. This bottle is very badly drawn. I see it! I see it! At the corner on the other side. In the middle something also is written, on the back. . .

While saying this Ossowiecki was drawing the figure (Page 90). Later on Dr. von Schrenck-Notzing asked in what language the words were written and Ossowiecki replied:

> In French. The bottle is a little inclined to one side. It has no cork. It is made up of several fine lines. There is first a brown envelope outside; then a greenish envelope and then a red envelope. Inside a piece of white paper folded in two with the drawing inside. It is written on a single sheet.

Dr. Dingwall subsequently opened the packet in view of the other investigators and pointed out the precautions he had taken against its being tampered with, over and above the fact that no opportunity to do this had been given. Dingwall stated that the supernormal character of the incident seemed quite decisive and that in his view coincidence could be wholly excluded.

In 1937 Sir Hubert Wilkins, well-known Australian explorer, was on his way to the Arctic, and a man with psychic abilities named Harold Sherman was in New York

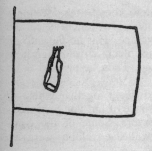

[Aug. 22. 1923]

Drawing by Dr. Dingwall.

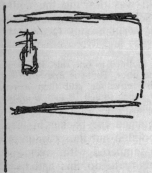

19 223

Drawing by Monsieur Ossowiecki.

City, writing down his mental impressions of the Wilkins trip. One day he wrote:

> You conferred in Ottawa with three important people. You may be delayed a week or more. Cheesman is with you—carries a good luck charm.

On that particular day Wilkins in Ottawa had conferred with three, no more, no less, important people. He had learned that he would be delayed for a week or more because of the radio in his plane. And Cheesman, a member of the expedition who was not with him at the moment but had gone on to Winnipeg, had that day been presented with a special good luck charm in the form of a wooden penguin.

Four hits, one miss—admittedly a bit beyond chance. And this sort of thing went on during Wilkins' whole trip.

As for the expedition—in 1937, at a time when U.S.-Russian official policy encouraged cooperation, an effort was made to establish an aeroplane route across the Arctic between the two countries. The third plane to attempt this crossing, with Sigismund Levanevsky and five companions, set out from Moscow on August 12th intending to make its first stop at Fairbanks, Alaska. Bad weather forced the plane off course and eventually came the message. . . "WE ARE GOING TO LAND. . ." and no more. Search parties, among whom were Sir Hubert Wilkins and his crew, set out immediately. In August Wilkins flew more than thirty thousand miles over the Arctic, but found no trace of Levanevsky. Still, the time the Russians had been lost was relatively short as Arctic survivals go, and so when the winter weather set in there was no question of abandoning the hunt. Wilkins was asked by the Soviet Government to continue. The explorer accordingly went back to New York to find another plane which could stand the winter rigors so near the North Pole.

Wilkins located the plane and all equipment except

certain direction-indicators for his short-wave radio. He decided he would have to fly back north without them. He writes in *Thoughts Through Space*:*

> This was disappointing, for it meant that if we came down on the ice, and, because of the weather or other difficulties, found it impossible to locate our exact position, others might have the same difficulty in locating us that we were having in our efforts to locate Levanevsky.

One night at their club Wilkins spoke of this disappointment to an acquaintance, Harold Sherman, with whom he had previously discussed their common interest in psychic phenomena. Sherman suggested that they try to communicate telepathically while Wilkins was away on his trip, and it was agreed upon. Three times a week at 11:30 p.m. Eastern Standard Time Wilkins was to concentrate on the figures expressing his latitude and longitude, while Sherman attempted to receive them.

Harold Sherman had previously had interesting telepathic experiences, but this was his first opportunity to experiment with his ESP talents under carefully controlled conditions, and he made the most of it. He wrote up each night's impressions in triplicate right after he received them. He then mailed one copy to Dr. Gardner Murphy, who was in New York City, and another copy to a skeptical friend, Samuel Emery. Thus he would have the U. S. post office cancellation marks as proof of the time that his material had been mailed.

Sherman writes:

> Wilkins had introduced me to Reginald Iversen, chief radio operator for the *New York Times*, with the thought that our experiments might be expedited by my turning over to Iversen copies of outstanding impressions, and letting him transmit them to Wilkins via short wave, so he could check for accuracy against his log and diary. However, as Iversen later testified, magnetic and sunspot conditions were so bad during the entire

---

*by Sir Hubert Wilkins and Harold M. Sherman, Creative Age Press, Inc., New York, 1942.

five months' period that he was able to contact Wilkins but thirteen times, and then only for short intervals.

This, as it turned out, was an act of providence insofar as the tests were concerned. For, with Wilkins almost entirely cut off from civilization, no scientific observer could offer the explanation that I, as the receiver, had had access to Wilkins through any possible physical medium.

What became evident as time went on was that while Wilkins was usually too busy to sit and concentrate at the given time three nights a week, Sherman was picking up vivid mental impressions of practically all of his strong thoughts in relation to the expedition no matter what time of day they were expressed. A good illustration of this occurred on the night of December 7th. Sherman writes:

I had no sooner seated myself in my study, at the appointed hour, and turned off the light, than I suddenly saw a fire flaring up against the black void of my inner mind.

The message he wrote that night and put into the mail to Murphy and Emery read as follows:

Don't know why, but I seem to see crackling fire shining out in the darkness of Aklavik—get a definite fire impression as though house burning—you can see it from your location on ice—I first thought it fire on ice near your tent, but impression persists it is white house burning and quite a crowd gathered around it—people running or hurrying toward flames—bitter cold—stiff breeze blowing.

It was not until February 14, 1938 that verification came from Wilkins. Aside from the fact that Sherman had not been aware that Wilkins had moved from Aklavik to Point Barrow, everything else was a perfect hit. At the very time when Wilkins was supposed to be sending his mental message to Sherman he had been diverted by a big fire which burned down a house in direct view from his window.

Sherman writes:

The fact that I had not sensed a change of location was interesting to me. Time or space apparently does not exist in telepathic communication. I had made contact with Wilkins' mind just as easily at Point Barrow as I had at Aklavik, but I had not felt the fact of his having physically moved from one point to another. Yet, as Wilkins told me later, allowing for the difference in time, he was seeing the fire taking place in Point Barrow, and I was writing down my impressions of it in New York City at the *same moment*!

This meant that, in some way which cannot as yet be entirely explained, I was attuned to Wilkins' mind, seeing and feeling, simultaneously, what he was seeing and feeling!

One of the most accurate and unusual accounts occurred on November 11th, while Wilkins was in Winnipeg still delayed in getting started on his Arctic trip. Sherman began by describing in detail an address which he believed Wilkins had made that day, and all the thoughts were similar to those Sir Hubert had actually expressed in an Armistice Day speech that morning. Then Sherman said:

> Someone seems to pin—or put something on the lapel of your coat—either pins a medal or a token of some kind. Someone gives you cigar.

The Mayor of Winnipeg had presented Wilkins with a badge of honor which a woman present had pinned on his coat. Then someone had presented him with a box of cigars.

> You are pleased with charcoal likeness. Tribute to Canadian war dead—flowers dropped from a plane. Something mechanical does not suit—de-icing—more extensive equipment. You in company with men in military attire—some women, evening dress—social occasion—important people present—much conversation. . . . YOU APPEAR TO BE IN EVENING DRESS YOURSELF.

An Arctic explorer in evening dress? But yes, as it turned out. And the other things were right too. A charcoal sketch of Wilkins had appeared in the paper on that day. He and his crew had left Winnipeg, hoping to start their northern flight, but had had to shorten their trip because of weather conditions. The de-icer on the propeller was not working satisfactorily. But while flying over Regina at about 11 a.m. they could see a procession of people carrying wreaths to lay at the Cenotaph. Wilkins writes:

> In the cockpit beside me were bunches of flowers given me by well-wishers as I left Winnipeg, and the thought occurred to me that it might be a suitable gesture if we were to circle over the Cenotaph and drop these flowers. I gave this some intense thought, but decided that as I was not a Canadian and had no personal association with Regina—had never even visited there —it might be a little presumptuous for me, conspicuously and without invitation, to take part in Regina's Armistice Day celebration.

Forced to land at Regina because of the weather, Wilkins received the same V.I.P. treatment there from the Mayor, who insisted that he must join the Chief of the Northwest Mounted Police as guest of honor at an Armistice Ball to be held that evening. This was a very formal affair, the main social event of the year at Regina. Sir Hubert tried to beg off because he didn't have evening clothes with him on the trip, not having expected to need them at the North Pole. But some were borrowed for him from an officer his size who was going to wear uniform. And so in Regina, Wilkins, like Cinderella, went to the ball in borrowed finery; and back in New York City Harold Sherman knew all about it telepathically.

Now, of course, the only check on Wilkins' statements was what he wrote in his diary. To suspect that he might have rearranged his records in order to produce a sensational story is certainly unwarranted. But, as has occurred with even such conscientious observers as Drs. J. B. Rhine and S. G. Soal, experiments must be airtight or their conclusions can be discredited. Thus we are fortunate that there were such verifications of Wilkins statements as the accounts which appeared in the newspapers of the cities he visited—accounts obviously not available to Sherman as he was writing and mailing his material in New York City.

There is also a statement, properly notarized, from a man who was extremely dubious about ESP at the beginning of the experiments:

This is to certify that I, Reginald Iversen, Radio Operator for the *New York Times*, was in contact with Harold Sherman off and on during the period of his telepathic tests with Sir Hubert Wilkins. It had been thought that some of Sherman's impressions could be checked by short wave with Wilkins and thus expedite the report on the tests, but magnetic and sun spot conditions were so bad during this entire time that I was unable to communicate with Sir Hubert Wilkins except on a comparatively few occasions.

On Monday evening, February 21, 1938, my wife and I visited Harold Sherman in his home and were present in his study at 380 Riverside Drive, New York City, when he was receiving impressions from Sir Hubert Wilkins, and, at that time, Mr. Sherman recorded the impression that Sir Hubert Wilkins was trying to get some messages through to me by short wave radio. I was dubious that this was so because Wilkins knew that the next two days, Tuesday and Wednesday, were my regular days off duty at the *Times*, and he rarely tried to contact me when he was certain that I was not on the job. But I learned the following morning that these messages had been received the night before by our night operator at the *Times*, who had tried to reach me by phone, and that the messages contained additional information which Harold Sherman had also telepathically received and recorded in my presence.

At no time during this period of six months did Harold Sherman ever seek such information as I might have known concerning Sir Hubert Wilkins and his activities in the far north. In fact, despite my skepticism, as it turned out, Sherman actually had a more accurate telepathic knowledge of what was happening to Wilkins in his search for the lost Russian fliers than I was able to gain in my ineffective attempts to keep in touch by short wave radio.

About the middle of March, Sherman began to have such feelings of exhilaration that he was sure Wilkins must be coming home. In fact, it was just at this time that the Russians had called off the unsuccessful expedition. Sherman, not knowing the time-table of Wilkins' departure from the Arctic continued his regular sittings and mailed in his reports for another ten days, but he wrote:

Would not surprise me to see you in New York as early as Saturday.

This also proved correct. To the rest of his remarkable paranormal information about the Arctic trip of his explorer friend, Harold Sherman had added a provocative bit of precognition.

9   *Does ESP Occur Spontaneously?*

November, 1864 Mrs. E. H. Elgee, on her way to join her
husband, Major Elgee, in India, was detained overnight
in Cairo. With her was a young lady referred to as Miss D.,
who was going to India to rejoin her parents. Obliged to
spend the night in a somewhat unfrequented hotel, they
were especially concerned for their safety, and after lock-
ing the door of their room they barricaded it with a chair
and a travelling bag. These, we presume, were the normal
precautions taken by 19th Century ladies travelling without escort.

Mrs. Elgee awoke from a sound sleep with the impression that someone had called her, and, sitting up in bed, to
her astonishment she saw the figure of a friend, whom she
thought to be in England. She says, "He appeared as if
most eager to speak to me, and I addressed him with,
'Good gracious! how did you come here?' So clear was the
figure that I noted every detail of his dress, even to three
onyx shirt studs which he always wore." He seemed to
approach Mrs. Elgee and then suddenly pointed across
the room. She turned and saw that Miss D. was sitting up
in her bed, gazing at the figure in terror. She then turned
her gaze back to her friend, who at this point faded
through the floor.

In the morning Mrs. Elgee and Miss D. compared
notes. They were convinced that the friend who visited
them in the night must be dead. Imagine Mrs. Elgee's
surprise, however, to learn later that he was not. Some
four years afterwards she met him and, without telling him
of her experience in Cairo, asked him if he could by any

chance remember what he had been doing on a certain night in November, 1864.

"Well," he said, "you do require me to have a good memory." After some reflection he recalled that on the night in question he had been thinking of Mrs. Elgee particularly, wishing he could go to her for advice.

Mrs. Elgee wrote her story to Edmund Gurney and it was published in the first edition of *Phantasms of the Living*. She had lost touch with Miss D. in the meantime; but when the book came out Miss D. read it and immediately sent her corroboration to Gurney.

This is a spontaneous case, one which occurred without any prearrangement. Such instances show that extra-sensory experiences do happen involuntarily, that they can be totally unexpected, and that on occasion they bring information which can later be verified. Another such incident is related by Mr. J. G. Keulemans, who was living in Paris in December, 1880, when there was an outbreak of smallpox. He sent his little son Isidore to London for safety, and there the child flourished.

On the morning of the 24th of January, 1881 Mr. Keulemans was awakened at half-past seven by the sound of Isidore's happy laughter. He saw a "bright, opaque, white mass" before his eyes and in the center of this light he saw his child's face, smiling. The apparition was too sudden and of too short duration to be called a dream, according to Mr. Keulemans, and too clear to be called an effect of the imagination.

"Thank God," he thought, hearing the child's sounds of delight, "little Isidore is happy as always."

Later, after a long walk and dinner with a friend, Keulemans saw the apparition of the child again, during an after dinner game of billiards. He was now seriously uneasy, and in spite of a subsequently reassuring letter that Isidore was in perfect health, he told his wife he was convinced that the child was dead. On the heels of the first letter came another, telling of Isidore's sudden illness and death, which had occurred at the exact time of the first apparition.

It was such cases as these, among other things, that engaged the attention of the Society for Psychical Research. The first major effort of this group soon after its inception in 1882 was a survey of spontaneous cases. Investigators hoped to get some idea of how frequently incidents of involuntary psychic phenomena really occur. They had all heard and read stories purporting to be true experiences; but were these isolated, or did they happen with relative frequency? The S.P.R. undertook to find out. A committee composed of Professor and Mrs. Sidgwick, Miss Alice Johnson, Frank Podmore, F. W. H. Myers and his brother Dr. A. T. Myers, began what they called a Census of Hallucinations.

The use of the word "hallucination" is an example of the extreme care always taken by the members of this organization not to commit themselves too deeply. Hallucinations are mental images that have sensory vividness but that are not caused, as sensations are, by stimulation of the sense organs. The dreams we have at night are oneiric hallucinations. Hallucinations occur frequently to certain types of insane people, and they occur to sane people during some illnesses, due to an unhealthy state of the body. Only a few hallucinations, whether oneiric or waking, are "veridical" in the sense of depicting objective occurrences, as ordinary sensory perceptions do.

The committee knew that ghosts and apparitions frequently were described as appearing completely external to the percipient, even as casting shadows. It also knew that such apparitions sometimes brought veridical information which was not previously known to the individual who saw them, such as that the person represented had grown a long beard before his death, or had turned white-headed since last seen by the percipient. Sometimes it had even been reported that a ghost brought news that another person was in trouble or was dead, which was later verified, as in the case of little Isidore.

Still, even taking all this into consideration, the committee protected itself by referring to all such apparitions as hallucinations. In order to explain its stand, the committee defined its use of the word hallucination as "telepathy of an externalized kind which appeared as an apparition." If hallucinations coincided with external events oftener than chance could account for, and if no normal causal relation could be suggested, then it inferred this would indicate telepathy in action. It thought that an agent telepathically impressed a percipient and the impression was projected in this dramatic visual form. In other words, an apparition was simply the objectified vehicle of a telepathic message or impulse. Nowadays, we would not define a hallucination in this manner, for we know more about the limits of telepathy.

Even so, the Census of Hallucinations was the first compilation of statistics regarding phenomena which had previously been ignored, or scoffed at. And its results were rather surprising, to say the least. Its evidence indicated, among other curious things, that the agent, the person seen as an apparition, could be either living or dead. The case of Mrs. Elgee just related reveals this fact, as did a variety of others. The census also showed that many people, otherwise sane and normal and well, do see ghosts. It will be for further generations to prove whether or not ghosts are the actual persons they purport to be, continuing to exist in some form not usually visible to the human eye, and able to communicate either their thoughts or appearances. At present, it can only be said that some spontaneous psychic phenomena present obstinate indications that such may be the case.

The first step of the Census of Hallucinations Committee was to circulate a questionnaire, worded so as to include only waking hallucinations of the three senses of sight, hearing, and touch. The question read:

> Have you ever, when believing yourself to be completely awake, had a vivid impression of seeing or being touched by a living being or inanimate object, or of hearing a voice; which impression, so far as you could discover, was not due to any external physical cause?

Printed on a form, the question could be answered Yes or No, and the person queried was asked to give his name, address, and occupation. Those who answered Yes were given another form which asked for details of their experiences. Answers were received from 17,000 people. Of these 15,316 replied No, and 1,684 replied Yes. The Yeses were 9.9 per cent of the total, so the Committee estimated from this that nearly 10% of the entire population probably have hallucinations.

A number of salient facts emerge from the Census of Hallucinations. One is that although apparitions are connected with other events besides death, they are more likely to be linked with death than with anything else. The Committee found that considerably more than chance was involved in the disproportionate number of death-coincidences. Visual hallucinations are the commonest, and this is noteworthy because in subjective hallucinations of the insane it is the auditory experiences which are most frequent. There was nothing to show that ill health or depression cause hallucinations of the sort described in this census, which proved quite different in character from the pink elephants and little green men of delirium or illness. They happen more to women than to men but infrequently to both. Most people have one, or at the most two, such experiences in a lifetime, if they have any at all. In roughly 9% of the cases, the manifestations were shared with others. This suggests a counter-hypothesis to the theory that hallucinations are only subjective: if seen by several persons together, an apparition would seem to consist of some-

102

thing physically present in space external to each observer. A glib rejoinder to this contention is "mass hallucination."

In conclusion, the Committee found:

> . . . that the distribution of recognized apparitions before, at, and after death of the person seen affords some argument for the continuity of psychical life and the possibilities of communication from the dead. . . The amount of evidence, however, does not appear to us to constitute anything like a conclusive case for post-mortem agency.

After the Census of Hallucinations appeared in the *Proceedings* of the S.P.R., there was a steady influx of spontaneous cases written in for the Society's files. Therefore the Committee, realizing that they would be analyzing such material for years, worked out a series of criticisms to keep themselves constantly on guard. About each case that came in they were to ask:

1. Is the account first hand?
2. Was it written or told before the corresponding event was known?
3. Has the principal witness been corroborated?
4. Was the percipient awake at the time?
5. Was the percipient an educated person of good character?
6. Was the apparition recognized?
7. Was it seen out of doors?
8. Was the percipient anxious or in a state of expectancy?
9. Could relevant details have been read back into the narrative after the event?
10. Could the coincidence between the experience and the event be accounted for by chance?

G. N. M. Tyrrell doesn't altogether agree with the basis of criticism painstakingly contrived by the Census Committee. He says:*

> It is evident that the value attached to a spontaneous case will depend enormously on individual judgment; anyone with a bias against such evidence will find plenty of ways in which he may attempt to explain it away. . . My own personal view is that the first-hand testimony of a reasonable witness is, on the

Apparitions, Society for Psychical Research, London, 1953.

whole, trustworthy unless special circumstances, such as the devices of a conjurer or prolonged strain on the attention, have been imposed on the witness. Second-hand evidence by reliable people, though less accurate than first-hand, is by no means valueless. . . A point often forgotten in the criticism of psychical phenomena is that, if serious criticism is being attempted, it is not enough to say in a general way that the evidence is insufficient to support a supernormal conclusion. Where a large number of carefully sifted and well-documented cases are concerned, this negative treatment is not enough. It is necessary to show that some normal explanation *will* reasonably fit each case.

For the purpose of systematic identification, the S.P.R. further grouped apparitions into four main classes. The first class comprises experimental cases in which the agent deliberately tries to project his material presence before an unsuspecting percipient, as in this experiment which succeeded on the first trial. The agent was Miss Edith Maughan (later Mrs. G. Rayleigh Vicars), and the account is taken from the *Proceedings* S.P.R.*

One night Miss Maughan was lying awake in bed reading. She had recently been studying with interest the various cases of astral projection in *Phantasms of the Living*, and made up her mind to try to project herself by force of will-concentration.

She lay back on her pillow with a resolute but half-doubtful and amused determination to make her friend in the next room, Miss Ethel Thompson, see her. After a few minutes she felt dizzy and only half-conscious. She says: "I don't know how long this state may have lasted, but I do remember emerging into a conscious state and thinking I had better leave off, as the strain had exhausted me."

As she blew out the candle to go to sleep she heard Miss Thompson, in the next room, raise her voice for a moment; but she did not distinguish more than the actual sound, and soon fell asleep.

The next morning Miss Thompson asked Miss Maughan if she had gone into her room to frighten her during the night. She declared that she had seemed to see her come in and bend over her and disappear immediately thereafter. It was at the approximate time when Miss Maughan was trying out her experiment.

*Vol. x, p. 273.

The following somewhat brazen invasion of privacy was not only successful the first time it was tried but was repeated with similar results on another occasion. Taken from *Phantasms of the Living,* vol. 1, pp 104-109, the case is reported by Mr. S. H. Beard.

On a certain Sunday evening in November, 1881, having been reading of the great power which the human will is capable of exercising, I determined with the whole force of my being, that I would be present in spirit in the front bedroom on the second floor of a house situated at 22 Hogarth Road, Kensington, in which room slept two ladies of my acquaintance, viz. Miss L.S.V. and Miss E.C.V., aged respectively 25 and 11 years. I was living at this time at 23 Kildare Gardens, a distance of about three miles from Hogarth Road, and I had not mentioned in any way my intention of trying this experiment to either of the above ladies, for the simple reason that it was only on retiring to rest upon this Sunday night that I made up my mind to do so. The time at which I determined I would be there was 1 o'clock in the morning, and I also had a strong intention of making my presence perceptible.

On the following Thursday I went to see the ladies in question, and in the course of conversation (without any allusion to the subject on my part) the elder one told me that on the previous Sunday night she had been much terrified by perceiving me standing by her bedside, and that she screamed when the apparition advanced towards her, and awoke her little sister, who saw me also. . . .

Besides exercising my power of volition very strongly, I put forth an effort which I cannot find words to describe. I was conscious of a mysterious influence of some sort permeating in my body, and had a distinct impression that I was exercising some force with which I had been hitherto unacquainted, but which I can now at certain times set in motion at will.

S.H.B.

Miss L. S. Verity and her sister E. S. Verity confirm that they both saw the apparition of S. H. B.

At Edmund Gurney's request, Mr. Beard wrote to him when he next intended to try an experiment. On March 22, 1884 he wrote to say that he would attempt an astral excursion that night. Miss Verity sent a letter a few days later verifying that she had not only seen his apparition while wide awake but that he had come forward and stroked her hair.

It is understood that Beard and Miss Verity were later married.

To the second class belong instances in which an apparition is seen, heard or felt at the time when the person represented by the apparition is undergoing some emergency. These instances are called crisis-cases or crisis-apparitions.

From Schlesien, Germany, Herr Karl Dignowity writes in 1889 that a friend of his, a brewer named Wünscher from a neighboring village, died of a sudden illness; but he had not heard of it. However, on the night of his death, Dignowity, having retired early, was awakened by what he thought was Wünscher's voice calling loudly outside his window. Then he saw Wünscher stride out from behind the linen press, wildly gesticulating with his arms as was his habit, and calling out, "What do you say to this? This afternoon at five o'clock I have died."

Startled by this information, Dignowity exclaimed, "Oh, that is not true!"

The apparition replied, "Truly, as I tell you; and what do you think? They want to bury me already on Tuesday afternoon at two o'clock."

During this conversation Dignowity examined himself to make sure he was not dreaming, and reassured himself that he was certainly awake. He admonished his friend to speak softly, so as not to wake and frighten his wife and child sleeping in the room; and Wünscher replied, "Don't be afraid, I will do no harm to your wife."

"If this be true that you have died," said Dignowity, "I am truly sorry for it; I will look after your children." Wünscher then stepped forward, stretched out his arms and moved his lips as though he would embrace Dignowity, who then said in a threatening tone, "Don't come so near, it is disagreeable to me." He lifted his right arm to ward him off, but before his arm reached the apparition it vanished.

The next day he learned that Wünscher had died that afternoon at five o'clock. He was buried on the following Tuesday at two.*

The instances cited so far in this chapter have been

Proceedings, S.P.R., vol. vi. p. 341.

old ones; but apparitions continue to appear in times of crisis, even to the present day. From the files of Dr. J. B. Rhine we learn that a little girl, playing with friends on an apartment house roof, was about to scramble over a dividing wall when, suddenly, she was confronted by a strange man wearing a blue, brass-buttoned uniform.

"Don't do that!" he said. Startled, the child stopped, just in time to save her life, for had she climbed over the wall she would have fallen five stories to the ground. The apparition spoke again. "I am Bill Johnson," it said. And then it disappeared.

The little girl went home and told her family about the incident. Then, for the first time, she learned that she was adopted, that the name of her deceased real father was Bill Johnson, and that he had been a railroad conductor who wore a blue uniform with brass buttons.

The third class includes cases in which a recognized apparition is seen or heard so long after the death of the person represented by the apparition that no coincidence with any crisis can be supposed. These are called post-mortem cases.

In the following instance* the apparition was seen by a man, his future wife, his little boy, and his dog. She apparently played the role of a Guardian Angel to the family for a time.

From St. Petersburg, Russia comes a letter dated April 29, 1891 from Eugene Mamtchitch telling about a girl whom he had known for several years before she died at the age of fifteen. Her name was Palladia and she was the daughter of a wealthy Russian landlord.

He says that in 1875, two years after her death, while in Kieff at a seance he heard taps and thought it was a joke. But at home he was able to communicate via alphabet with Palladia. She said: "Replace the angel, it is falling." He visited her grave, found it buried under snow, with the marble statue of an angel with cross quite askew.

Proceedings S.P.R., vol. x. pp. 387-91.

Later she appeared to him, and after that she appeared frequently. On rare occasions she gave a warning or announcement.

Once in 1879 he spoke to her. He suddenly saw her looking at him with joy and serenity. He asked, "What do you feel?"

"Peace," she answered.

"I understand," he replied.

The young lady whom he later married saw her one day while visiting in his home. She was told, "Don't be afraid of me, I am good and affectionate."

Mr. Mamtchitch's setter dog ran in fright once when she appeared, and his little son also saw her. The child's face was peaceful and happy, for he was not frightened by her.

The Reverend C. T. Forster, Vicar of Hinxton, sent in the following account of the sighting of a Mrs. de Fréville the night of her death.* He says:

My late parishioner, Mrs. de Fréville, was a somewhat eccentric lady, who was specially morbid on the subject of tombs, etc.

The Vicar learned that Alfred Bard, a gardner who had once been in her employ, had seen her in the graveyard on the night of May 8th. She had died in London on the afternoon of May 8th, but the news did not reach Hinxton until the following morning. Bard had seen her leaning with her elbows on the palisade, with cloak and bonnet on, between nine and ten that night. "I turned again to look at her and she was gone," he told his wife Sarah.

Forster writes that Bard gave him a very clear and circumstantial account of what he had seen. "He is a man of great observation," he said, "being a self-taught naturalist, and I am quite satisfied that he desires to speak the truth without any exaggeration."

F. W. H. Myers has quoted this case in *Human Personality and Its Survival of Bodily Death,* explaining it as follows:

The incident suggests that Bard had come upon Mrs. de Fréville's spirit, so to say, unawares. One cannot imagine that

Phantasms of the Living, vol. i., p. 212.

she specially wished him to see her, and to see her engaged in what seems so needless and undignified a retracing of currents of earthly thought. Rather this seems a rudimentary *haunting*—an incipient lapse into those aimless, perhaps unconscious, reappearances in familiar spots which may persist (as it would seem) for many years after death.

This leads us into class four of the Census of Hallucinations—genuine "ghosts," or apparitions which habitually haunt certain places. It may surprise the reader to learn that real hauntings seldom take on the coloration of those of fiction. Real ghosts almost never run around moaning and dragging chains. And the usual presumption that some great crime or catastrophe is always to be sought in the background of a haunt is not necessarily so. Mrs. de Fréville was concerned in no tragedy; she was merely an elderly lady with a fancy for sepulchres.

In fact, a typical haunting is almost dull. In the *Journal* S.P.R.* an account was given by Miss M. W. Scott of an apparition seen several times by herself, and occasionally by others, on a country road near her home. Her first experience was in May, 1892, when, walking down a short incline on her way home, she saw a tall man dressed in black a few yards in front of her. He turned a corner of the road, and there suddenly disappeared. On following him around the corner, Miss Scott found her sister, who had just seen a tall man dressed in black, whom she took for a clergyman, coming to meet her on the road. She had looked away for a moment, and on glancing back could see no one anywhere near. Miss Scott's sister was gazing up and down the road in much bewilderment. It appeared that they had not seen the man at exactly the same moment nor in quite the same place, but from their description of him, it was obviously the identical person. It seemed impossible that a real man could have been where he was and then disappeared so suddenly.

*Vol. VI., p. 146, November, 1893.

Does ESP Occur Spontaneously?

In August, 1900 Miss Scott wrote that she had seen her apparition again, twice. By then she had almost forgotten the existence of her supernatural neighbor, when there he was, walking ahead of her as before. She tried to catch up to him, but instantly he vanished. He had been dressed the same way as when last seen eight years before.

Most other haunts who were carefully observed and reported by the S.P.R. seemed only to wander in familiar scenes. Even the famous Morton ghost, carefully observed over a period of years, never did anything but walk about the house in which she had previously lived, and stand in her favorite bow window. This raises a definite point of distinction between crisis-apparitions, who might very likely indicate the actual deceased personality himself rushing in with a message or a warning, and hauntings. Myers considers that the latter may be merely what he calls veridical after-images, meaning that some kind of image of a person is left in areas he had previously frequented, particularly if he felt strong emotions at the time.

An interesting elaboration on this idea was given by automatic writing when Miss A., whom we have mentioned earlier, was communicating with an alleged entity who had established herself to the satisfaction of Lord and Lady Radnor as a relative named Estelle.

Estelle wrote: You ask me whom I see in this habitation. I see so many shades and several spirits. I see also a good many reflections. Can you tell me if there was a child died upstairs? Was there an infant who died rather suddenly? Because I continually see the shadow of an infant upstairs, near the room where you dress.

Lord Radnor says: An infant brother of mine died of convulsions in a nursery which then occupied the part of the house where the figure of the baby was said to have appeared. I do not see any way in which Miss A. could have known either of the death of my infant brother or of the fact that that part of the house had previously been a nursery. "What do you mean by a shadow?" he asked.

Estelle went on: Yes, it is only a shadow. A shadow is when any one thinks so continually of a person that they imprint

110

their shadow or memory on the surrounding atmosphere. In fact, they make a form; and I myself am inclined to think that so-called ghosts, of those who have been murdered, or who have died suddenly, are more often shadows than earthbound spirits; for the reason that they are ever in the thoughts of the murderer, and so he creates, as it were, their shadow or image.

Myers thinks the curious question as to the influence of certain *houses* in generating apparitions may be included under the broader heading of *retrocognition*— clairvoyant perception by some psychic person of past activities in the house. "Manifestations," he says, "which occur in haunted houses depend, let us say, on something which has taken place a long time ago."

Are they a sequel, he wonders, or only a residue? Is there fresh operation going on, or only fresh perception of something already accomplished? Unfortunately for research, the "progressive" modern world leaves us with fewer and fewer old houses in which genuine hauntings may be observed.

We still have our spontaneous ESP occurrences, however, as we did long before the S.P.R. began to collect and examine them; and they continue to happen much more frequently than is commonly realized. Mention the subject to your elevator man, or to the lady next door. If they haven't a personal experience to relate, very likely they know someone who does.

The writer has discovered this for herself. I became curious about extrasensory perception and psychic phenomena some years ago, and for a long time I read about the subject and studied it, but seldom mentioned it. I didn't want to be asked, "What are you—some kind of a nut?" Now I have learned that, far from labelling me weird, people are more likely to show interest and ask questions, if I bring the subject up. And here's the fascinating thing: many I talk to have had psychic experiences of their own. They were as reluctant as I to speak of it, but when I broke the ice they frequently topped my stories with much better ones of their own.

The experience may have been simple and uncomplicated. A friend of mine once heard her deceased father's voice just at the moment when she most needed encouragement. Only her name was spoken, but with her father's own inflection, and it cheered her immeasurably.

Or the story may be more involved, like that of Mrs. F. and Mrs. A., a mother and daughter, who were stopped in their car one night by the apparition of their husband and father holding up his hand and blocking their way. When, impressed by the warning, they left the car and walked cautiously ahead on the road, they discovered around the next bend that the old, back-country bridge had collapsed.

You might hear such stories as the one about the woman who had an inexplicable urge to call a friend on the telephone. It was late at night and she had nothing important to impart, but still she felt strongly compelled to make the call. When, after numerous rings, the friend answered the phone, she was groggy from escaping gas in her apartment. If she had not been awakened by the telephone call, she would have been asphyxiated.

Then there was the little ten-year-old Utah boy whose mother wrote his unhappy story to Dr. Louise E. Rhine He said one morning, "Oh, Mom, I had a terrible dream last night. A car ran me down. It was so awful!" His mother uttered a silent prayer, and admonished him to stay on the sidewalk; but just three minutes after he had left for school a truck ran up on the sidewalk and struck and killed him.

Another story from Mrs. Rhine's file speaks of a young woman who, one night, was asked by an acquaintance about her four-year-old daughter. The mother took from her purse a small picture of the little girl. The friend looked at it with interest and then said, rather fancifully, it would seem, "That child should have a musical education. It would be to her a book of gold with notes of silver for her in it."

Surprised by her friend's seriousness, the mother thought again and again of the suggestion. When she got home the little girl was asleep. As soon as the child awoke the next morning she began to search for something, among her bedcovers, and then on the dresser and in the drawers. Her mother asked her what she was looking for.

"I want the book of gold with something in it for me," the little girl said.

If you do start looking about to collect ESP stories from your friends, you will find some that don't stand up to scrutiny. It will surprise you to learn that some individuals you know are so taken in by what, to you, is obviously their own desire to believe. One of the main reasons why Spiritualism has received so little recognition is because of the naivéte of so many of the people attached to it. They accept everything without reservation—the more preposterous it is, the more credulous they are, particularly if the ESP deals with survival of bodily death. Explorers of the World Beyond will flock to a Spiritualist camp where fraudulent materializations have been publicly exposed. They still will not believe they have been deceived even when faced with photographic evidence—exposures on infra-red film that show someone's etheric beloved to have actually been a grossly flesh and blood medium draped in gossamery cheesecloth.

Once convinced by what may have been genuine ESP, these persons are reluctant to dismiss any further experiences which come their way. I know one woman of convincing psychic talent whose specialty is what she terms spirit photography. On occasion she has taken pictures which show unexplainable rods and circles, conceivably of supernormal origin. She also makes an occasional double exposure, as any careless photographer might do.

But rather than admit they are simple errors, she accepts the double outlines she sees and the faces superimposed on other faces as genuine spirit photographs.

For the budding investigator, discrimination is a basic requisite, and it must be maintained no matter how carried away he becomes in his quest—especially so as he gets more deeply involved. Too many eager seekers never read books critical or analytical of psychical phenomena, but only those which are philosophical or mystical or "personal experience" kinds of things. They can see no possible reason for investigating or testing for proof. "It happened to me and so I believe," they say, and that's the end of it. Sir Arthur Conan Doyle is an example of a man of high intelligence who became so captivated by his findings that he lost all critical sense. Conan Doyle came to accept so completely spirit communication that he took everything without question, no matter how obvious the chicanery.

At the other extreme are those parapsychologists who inflexibly disparage everything and everyone who does not have an approach as objective as their own. They consume their energy writing erudite papers for the consideration of their fellow researchers in academic terms intelligible to none but their colleagues. They are so confined by laboratory-devised statistical analyses that they ignore many of the best indications of ESP—because they originate from enthusiasts who show insufficient critical sense. Psychical researchers, in order not to fall flat on their faces as "ghost chasers," have always fallen over backwards from fear of being considered as bizarre as the topic with which they deal.

Fortunately, there is also a happy medium—with hardly any pun intended. There are intelligent people who can take the subject or leave it alone, although they prefer to take it. They are normal, average, rational individuals with questioning minds. They may have had some personal psychic experience or they may have attended a seance where some information was given them, so private that they feel no trickery could have produced it. Or they may be like the train of little ladies in the Mikado "wondering what the world can be" and not want to overlook that portion of it taken over by the supernormal.

Once their interest is aroused, these inquiring individuals read books on extrasensory perception and related subjects, and discusses ESP with other persons of like mind. They may even come to favor a belief that survival of bodily death has been proved. But they resent being called credulous or gullible or plain simple because after careful argument and consideration they support this opinion. All fields of discovery have been indebted to men and women of this type and they produce many of the best psychical researchers.

Whichever of these categories you fit into, you will probably wish to know how best to judge the cases of ESP which come under your observation. The value of a case to an ambitious investigator can be simply estimated by following J. Fraser Nicol's three points of critique:

1. That the experience be veridical, i.e., that it relate to an actual event that was occurring, had occurred, or would occur.
2. That there be an independent witness who testifies that the percipient related his experience to him before he came to know, by normal means, that the experience had been veridical, and
3. That no more than five years have passed between the experience and the written account of it.

With these points to judge by, let us examine some stories from the records of psychical research, although the authenticating material is not always here included.

Does ESP Occur Spontaneously?

We will begin with an old case, because it seems to indicate so well the action of telepathy:

The Reverend P. H. Newnham of Devonport, England writes* that in March, 1861 his wife was confined to her bed at home in Houghton because of illness. One day, walking through a lane, he found the first wild violets of the spring and took them home to her. He never told her the specific place where he had picked the violets, nor did he ever walk there with her, for they left that town shortly thereafter. In 1873, twelve years later, they visited friends in Houghton, and the Reverend Newnham and his wife went out for a walk. They happened to go up the lane in question, and as they passed the place he began to think about having picked violets there for his wife, although now the ground about the hedges had been grubbed and no flowers grew there. At that moment his wife said, "It's very curious, but if it were not impossible, I should declare that I could smell violets in the hedge."

Another and much more modern instance of telepathy is related by Betty and Fraser Nicol in *Tomorrow* Magazine.*

It occurred in Boston in the late afternoon of June 14, 1955. Jack Sullivan, a welder, was alone in a fourteen foot trench on Washington Street, and everyone else on the job had gone home. Sullivan pulled a welding shield down over his face and started to weld some pipe sections together when tons of earth, clay and stone fell upon him as the trench caved in.

He was knocked down against the pipe in a more or less kneeling position with his legs doubled under him. His head was thrown against the pipe, his nose was smashed against the inside of the welding mask. His shoulder was jammed against the red hot weld he had been making on the pipes, and he couldn't move to relieve the intense pain he was suffering from it.

The article goes on: "Though buried under the earth, he shouted for help, hoping the children might still be around and hear. But after a few shouts he became short of breath. He thought it best to take things easily and not use up the air around the mask too quickly. With the generator running on the truck, probably no one could hear him anyhow, he realized."

Then a vivid picture of his best friend and fellow worker, Tommy Whittaker, came into his mind. He knew that Whittaker

*Phantasms of the Living, vol. 1.
*Vol. 5, No. 3, Spring, 1957.

was working that day on another part of the water-main project some four or five miles away. Sullivan got the idea that Tommy Whittaker might help him, and he had a very clear mental picture of his friend.

Whittaker didn't even know that Sullivan was at the Washington Street job, but into his vacant mind as he worked at his welding that afternoon came the idea that he must go up to the Washington Street job and see if everything was all right. His feeling was so vague he could not explain it, but he felt that something was wrong. He left his work and made his way as quickly as possible to Washington Street, and there he saw one of his company's trucks standing with the generator running. As he drew up behind it, and then walked to the trench, he saw the cavein, and Sullivan's hand sticking out of the dirt. Sullivan was soon rescued because of his telepathic message, after having been buried for about an hour.

An incident which might be credited to spontaneous general extrasensory perception is quoted in *Hidden Channels of the Mind*:

A woman watching television had a sudden strong compulsion to call home. Not even waiting until the end of the program, she telephoned her mother. "My mother answered," she says, "and immediately broke into sobs of relief. 'Why, Virginia, I've been trying to reach you for thirty minutes. The operator was unable to trace your new number. I've been sitting here by the phone, wondering how in the world I could reach you to tell you Dad suffered a heart attack and is in the hospital.'"

Dr. Gordon Seagrave in his book *Burma Surgeon Returns** cites an example of precognition: "Early on the morning of May 17, 1944, I was tossing sleeplessly on my bed, wishing it were time to get up. . . . One of those incredible hunches hit me. Something was cooking. I hustled the boys out of bed and ordered them to evacuate all our remaining patients to the Chinese regimental hospital. While they emptied the wards, our few Chinese, our Burmese boys, and I pulled the tents down and rolled them up. When the trucks returned we loaded them with equip-

*W. W. Norton & Co., Inc., p. 132.

ment for a surgical hospital. Everyone thought the Old Man had gone mad."

But the Old Man had anticipated just what was needed. After breakfast came the utterly unexpected orders to evacuate the hospital with all possible speed.

Along the line of precognition, William O. Stevens in *Psychics and Common Sense** tells of a personal friend of his, a distinguished actor and director, who had the following experience in World War I, during his tour of duty in India:

> In the course of parachute instruction the future distinguished actor and director had made several jumps and rather enjoyed the experience. However, one morning as he walked across the landing field toward the aeroplane from which he was to jump, he had a sudden feeling of, as he called it—repulsion—come over him, and he stopped dead in his tracks.
>
> At first his Flight Commander teased him, for he had a fine record, but he absolutely refused to go up. Then the Flight Commander *ordered* him to get into the aeroplane. Offering to go up in another but not in that one, the young soldier continued to refuse and stood firm to the point of being arrested for insubordination. From prison he learned that the aeroplane which he had held in disfavor had crashed and all on board had been killed. Now he was suspected of knowing that something had been wrong with the plane. He was disgraced and deprived of his rank. It was three years before he was able to clear himself and work back up. He was later commissioned.

Sometimes precognition comes in the form of a dream. The following story was one of those received by the American Society for Psychical Research.*

> Mrs. Antoinette Terlingo of Clifton Heights, Pennsylvania, in a letter dated February 25, 1957, related that she had dreamed she saw her father dead in a coffin, but only his head and shoulders were visible. Around his neck was a white turkish towel. His doctor, who was a woman, said it was better to have him embalmed now. Mrs. Terlingo awoke screaming, sure that her father had died. He had been a patient for seven years at the Newton D. Baker Veteran's Hospital in Martinsburg, W.

*E. P. Dutton & Co., Inc., New York, 1953.
Ibid.

Va.; but the last time the family had heard from him he was "feeling fine, a little tired, but okay."

Less than two weeks later Mrs. Terlingo and her mother were called to the hospital, where her father had had a stroke. They found him with a portable oxygen mask on, and a white turkish towel around his neck, as in the dream. After he died the next day, his doctor—a new one—who was the first woman doctor he had ever had, told them that before taking him to Pennsylvania for burial they should have him embalmed, as there was a law of which they were unfamiliar that a corpse cannot otherwise be taken across a state line. When Mrs. Terlingo finally saw her father in his coffin, the last piece of the dream puzzle fell into place. He was draped with the United States flag up to his chest, and only his head and shoulders were visible.

On occasion some of our best ESP data is brought us by ghosts or apparitions. Helen Simpson Phillips, the retired nurse whose psychic experiences are spoken of in an earlier chapter, has a story to relate regarding a spontaneous vision in which she received evidential information about, or from, her uncle. Helen and her sister were vacationing in Florida, when, one afternoon, the wall of their hotel room suddenly seemed to change into a movie screen for Helen. While the picture unfolded before her, she watched enthralled as her Uncle Henry appeared, working in his Virginia fields.

As she kept her eyes glued to the wall, a gypsy from a nearby camp came up behind her uncle and stole a lamb, and while he was sneaking away Uncle Henry saw him and chased after him. They wrestled on the bank of the river and the dirt crumbled away, sending them both into the stream. The gypsy swam to safety, but Uncle Henry, after struggling in the water, sank.

Helen said to her sister, as the vision faded, "Uncle Henry has been drowned."

"Oh, Helen," said her prosaic sister, to whom a wall was merely a wall, "be sensible."

But in a few days a newspaper was received from their

home, reporting that their Uncle Henry had been found in the river, presumably a suicide. Then psychically sensitive Helen knew why she had been shown the picture. She immediately wrote the details incident to his death to his distraught wife, explaining that Uncle Henry had come to her in a vision so that his wife could be reassured.

And finally, if the following spontaneous experience of Edgar Wallace, the most successful writer of detective stories since Conan Doyle, does not put him in the same psychical category as Sir Arthur, at least it makes him a member of the club. It is quoted in *The Haunted Mind* by Nandor Fodor.*

> On the night of May 10, 1931, Wallace was sitting at his desk writing a vitriolic attack against Hannen Swaffer, a somewhat flamboyant British newspaper man, and his championship of Spiritualism. In the stillness of the night Wallace heard a voice.
> "I think that is very silly and you ought to be ashamed of yourself."
> There was no one in the room with Wallace. The voice repeated, "It *is* silly."
> "What is silly?" the writer asked, considerably rattled. There was no answer.
> To regain his composure Wallace went into his wife's room, leaving the manuscript on which he had been working on his desk, with his watch and chain on top of it. When he returned, the writing had disappeared and the watch and chain had been moved.
> At five o'clock in the morning a still more amazing event took place. Wallace was awakened by his own coughing and got up to make a cup of tea. He saw in the corner of his study, sitting in a chair, a woman whom he recognized instantly. She was Hannen Swaffer's dead sister-in-law, whom Wallace had known well. She looked perfectly natural and they carried on a long conversation. Then she faded out.
> For the record, Edgar Wallace made a solemn statement after this revealing night. Said he: "I shall no longer sneer at spirits."

*Helix Press, New York, 1959.

10   *Who Believes in ESP?*

experience, or "it really happened to *me!*", the most impressive argument for ESP as a hardworking phenomenon is a survey of its appearance among the great and famous. Though some of these distinguished individuals have encountered even the mildest telepathy with great misgivings, disclosing the occurrence only with reluctance, others have relished ghosts, poltergeists, and even seance manifestations with the same gusto with which they embraced all new adventures.

Samuel Clemens, the beloved Mark Twain, whose enthusiasm for life surmounted his many sorrows from the loss of those he loved, joined the Society for Psychical Research with a letter declaring that "Thought transference, as you call it, or mental telegraphy as I have been in the habit of calling it, has been a very strong interest with me for the past nine or ten years."

With his reliable sense of humor working perhaps a little overtime, Twain proposed to the S.P.R. a plan to simplify communication:

> In my own case it has often been demonstrated that people can have crystal-clear mental communication with each other over vast distances. Doubtless to be able to do this the two minds have to be in a peculiarly favorable condition for the moment. Very well, then, why shouldn't some scientist find it possible to invent a way to *create* this condition of *rapport* between two minds at will? Then we should drop the slow and cumbersome telephone and say, "Connect me with the brain of the chief of police at Peking." We shouldn't need to know the man's language; we should communicate by thought only, and say in a couple minutes what couldn't be inflated into words in

an hour and a half. Telephones, telegraphs and words are too slow for this age; we must get something that is faster.

Truly yours,
S. L. Clemens*

After the personal experiences he had with ESP, it is not much wonder that Mark Twain was an advocate of telepathy. His dream before his brother's death has already been mentioned. In *Thoughts Through Space* Harold Sherman tells us that in the year 1906 Mark Twain wanted to refer to an article written by him for the *Christian Union* and published in 1885. He searched his files, but could not find a copy. The material was needed for the basis of a new series of articles, but even the office of the publication could give him no help. Once more Clemens went exhaustively through all his papers, to no avail.

The next day he was walking down Fifth Avenue in New York City. While he was waiting to cross Forty-second Street, a stranger rushed up to him and pressed some clippings into his hand.

"I've been saving these for more than twenty years," he said, "but this morning it occurred to me to send them to you. I was going to mail them, but now that I see you I'll hand them to you."

Mark Twain thanked the man, who disappeared into the crowd, and then he looked at the clippings. They were the very ones he had been so anxious to find—from the *Christian Union* of 1885.

Dr. Oliver Wendell Holmes, one of America's most distinguished men of letters as well as a Doctor of Medicine, and a professor of anatomy and physiology, wrote of his own clairvoyant incident in *Over the Tea Cups*. One night at dinner he happened to think of a curious court case of which he had read many years before. He told the ladies present of Abraham Thornton who, in 1817, had been let off from a charge of murder because of an

Journal S.P.R., Vol. 1, 1884.

old law still in force, known as "trial by battel." He threw down his glove and it was not taken up by the brother of his victim, and so by law he was released.

After telling this story, Holmes arose from dinner, and found that the mail from England had arrived. In it was a letter from a man named Frederick Rathbone which started out:

> Dear Sir, In travelling the other day I met with a reprint of the very interesting case of Thornton for murder, 1817. The prisoner pleaded successfully the old Wager of Battel. I thought you would like to read the account, and send it with this . . .

Oliver Wendell Holmes says of this occurrence:

> I consider the evidence of entire independence, apart from possible "telepathic" causation, completely waterproof, air-tight, incombustible, and unassailable.

The poet Percy Bysshe Shelley had several visual hallucinations notably significant. In the last one, he saw Allegra, the late daughter of Lord Byron. She seemed to rise from a bay in the sea and clasp her hands in joy, smiling at him. Two months later Shelley was drowned in this same bay.

Authors—who are constantly asked where on earth do they get their ideas—have been known to receive plots or characterizations from supernormal sources. Robert Louis Stevenson used to dream the plots of his stories with the help of those he referred to as "the little people" who managed his "internal theatre." "These little people, these Brownies," he said, "can tell me a story piece by piece, like a serial and keep *me,* its supposed creator, all the while in total ignorance of where they aim."

Charles Dickens once dreamed of meeting a certain lady, Miss Napier by name, whom he did not know. A few days later he *was* presented to a charming stranger who looked exactly like the girl of his dream, and her name was Miss Napier.

Who Believes in ESP?

Victor Hugo's extrasensory claim was that on occasion he was possessed by the spirit of Molière, who, he stoutly maintained, frequently guided his pen.

Count Maurice Maeterlinck, author of *The Blue Bird,* and winner of the Nobel Prize in Literature in 1911, was interested in the paranormal all his life; but his greatest excitement along this line was not subjective but objective. He travelled as an interested observer to witness the amazing Elberfeld horses. These horses had been trained by a man who believed that animals can think, and who appeared to have succeeded in proving it. He taught his horses to express themselves by tapping with their hooves. They achieved the point where they independently answered questions and solved mathematical problems. Many investigators of high intelligence and objectivity have admitted themselves completely stumped by these horses, who have gone down in the history of psychical research as a great and unexplained enigma. Of them Maeterlinck wrote: "I could not have been more astonished if I had suddenly heard a voice of the dead. . . We seek in vain for explanation; and nothing delivers us from the burden of this mystery."

Modern author Stuart Cloete once in Africa heard the ghost of a galloping horse, but he did not see it. And MacKinlay Kantor, author of recent best-seller *Spirit Lake,* and the classic *The Voice of Bugle Ann*, once had the covers pulled from him in bed by an unseen force which he could account for no other way than ghostly.

Another Nobel Prize winner, author Thomas Mann, had his most telling psychic experience by way of a seance room, when the astounding Rudi Schneider was under close examination. Mann held the entranced medium's wrists while his knees were controlled by another witness. Mann wrote of it:

Finally the thing that from all evidence was not possible nevertheless took place! May I be struck by lightning if I'm

124

lying! Before my eyes, which were free of any kind of influence and were equally disposed to see nothing if there weren't anything to see, the thing occurred; not once but repeatedly.

What Mann saw was a clawlike hand shaking the draperies, a bell floating in mid-air ringing and being tossed about the room, a typewriter typing by invisible means, and other irregularities of like nature. The medium and his surroundings had been carefully gone over to insure that no trickery was possible. Mann went on:

> After having seen for myself, I consider it my duty to testify that, by any human estimation, all possibility of mechanical fraud, prestidigitation or illusionism must be excluded from the experience in which I participated. What, in sum, did I see? Two-thirds of my readers will reply, "Charlatanism, sleight of hand, hoax." Some day, however, when our knowledge of these things will have progressed, when this realm becomes broadly known, they will deny having uttered such a judgment.

A contemporary Shakespeare (to whom, by the way, every variety of psychic phenomena provided dramatic material), the poet and playwright Ben Jonson, had an unhappy vision which is reported by the Scottish poet William Drummond:

> At that tyme the pest was in London; he [Jonson] being in the country with old Cambden, he saw in a vision his eldest son, then a child and at London, appear unto him with the mark of a bloodie cross in his forehead, as if it had been cutted with a sword, at which amazed he prayed unto God, and in the morning he came to Mr. Cambden's chamber to tell him; who persuaded him it was but an apprehension of his fantasie, at which he should not be disjected; in the mean tyme came then letters from his wife of the death of that boy in plague. He appeared to him (he said) of a manly shape, and of that grouth that he thinks he shall be at the resurrection.

Fulton Oursler, reporter, drama critic, editor, in the course of time became profoundly impressed by the co-incidence between details of certain of his dreams and the events which usually occurred within twenty-four hours afterwards. One dream in particular in which he saw blood all over his house came true in exact detail the next afternoon when his dog was run over by a car and brought inside for first aid.

Edward William Bok tells a story on himself in *Twice Thirty*. The longtime publisher of the *Ladies Home Journal* was at a large luncheon of publishers and editors and was listening to the man next to him relate a story "when suddenly there appeared before me as plainly as if she were in the flesh my wife's mother," he says, "who had passed away two years before. It was just such a gathering as she would have enjoyed, and, radiant in smiles, she began a series of questions to which I gave answer, and began describing her state of wonderful happiness. The next thing I knew I felt a hand on my shoulders and heard: 'Well, how about it?' " Bok came awake from his period of abstraction and was told, "You just didn't seem to be here." But where had he been? He learned afterwards that the story he was supposed to have been listening to had lasted five minutes.

Both Hamlin Garland, Pulitzer prizewinner, and Stewart Edward White wrote numerous books on their interest in psychical research. Thomas Sugrue, whose life of the reluctant psychic Edgar Cayce, is called *There is a River,* Kenneth Roberts, who concerned himself with dowsing, and Mary Roberts Rinehart, the foremost woman writer of detective fiction, were all brushed with the invisible wing of psi. Renting an apartment in Washington, D. C. which had previously been occupied by a defunct, somewhat gross member of the U. S. Congress, Mrs. Rinehart found herself contending with an all-too-vigorous poltergeist, ostensibly the late Senator.

Albert Payson Terhune, dog lover, Pierre van Paassen, whose *Days of Our Years* described the activities of an unfriendly ghost dog, and H. Rider Haggard, the author of *She,* all have psychic incidents to tell about their pets. Haggard's dog, which had wandered off and been killed by a train, is supposed to have appeared to his master to report his death.

To conclude the list of literary lights, William Butler Yeats, one of the most literary, was also one of the most impetuous devotees of psychical matters. In an article entitled "The Psychic World of W. B. Yeats"* Sherman Yellen writes:

> William Butler Yeats, the great modern poet, has long been an embarrassment to many among his large and admiring following. In the twenty-two years following his death, Yeats's reputation as our century's greatest poet remains unchallenged. Biographers have devoted themselves to the multi-faceted aspects of their subject and we have been given incisive portraits of Yeats the poet, Yeats the dramatist, Yeats the Irish statesman, Yeats the folklorist, and Yeats the lover. But Yeats, the staunch advocate of psychic research and occult realities, remains to this day the subject of the conspiratorial wink and the indulgent apology.

The psychic concerns of Yeats, Yellen says, are viewed as part of the eccentric and old-fashioned furniture of his mind, a weakness in an otherwise unblemished genius. Yellen points to a review in *Time** which said that:

> Yeats was a genius, probably the twentieth century's greatest poet. But his private life and personal beliefs were filled with quirks and oddities, mystical beliefs and spiritual devotions. . . Merely to contemplate what Yeats seriously believed in is enough to stagger the modern reader. He had, or vowed he had, complete faith in ghosts, fairies, magic, table rapping, and Spiritualism.

Yet Yellen maintains that:

> It was Yeats' fundamental honesty, rather than his practical fancy, that led him to psychical research. As an observer of the psychic wonders of the seance room, Yeats was often both gullible and inept, but as a personal experimenter in the field, he was part of the growing movement toward a scientific examination and experiment with the psychic . . .

Tomorrow Magazine, Vol. 10, No. 1, Winter, 1962.
*June 16, 1961.

Who Believes in ESP?

Surprised by his own sudden display of ESP was Arthur James Balfour, Prime Minister of England from 1903-05. His sister Eleanor had married Henry Sidgwick, the first president of the S.P.R. and she was one of its most energetic members. His brother Gerald was also active in the Society. He had another sister who looked into a crystal ball and told them what she saw. Arthur Balfour himself would have none of it. But when he laughingly looked in his sister's crystal one day, his expression quickly changed. For within the crystal was a scene, and he could identify the person and place. He recognized a friend, Miss Grant, seated at her home, at tea. On the Tuesday following he met Miss Grant and told her:

> On Sunday at five o'clock, you were seated under a standard lamp making tea. A man in blue serge was beside you; his back was towards me. I saw the tip of his moustache. You were wearing a certain dress that I have never seen you wear. (And he described the dress.)
>
> "Were the blinds up?" asked Miss Grant.
>
> "I do not know; I was at St. Andrew's," said Lord Balfour. The lady admitted the facts were correct and she and Balfour wrote out and signed a report of the incident.*

Luther Burbank wrote in *Hearst's* Magazine for May, 1923:

> I inherited my mother's ability to send and receive communications. So did one of my sisters. In tests before representatives of the University of California she was able, seven times out of ten, to receive messages sent to her telepathically. My mother, who lived to be more than ninety-six years of age, was in poor health the last years of her life. During these years I often wished to summon my sister. On such occasions I never had to write, telephone or telegraph to her. Instead, I sent her messages telepathically, and each time she arrived in Santa Rosa, Calif., where I lived, on the next train.

Woman suffragist Susan B. Anthony had a dream which very likely saved her life. It was recounted by Miss

---

Noted Witnesses for Psychic Occurrences by Dr. Walter Franklin Prince, Boston Society for Psychic Research, Boston, 1928.

Anthony's intimate friend, Mrs. Elizabeth Cady Stanton, who wrote in her diary:*

> In a few days we are expecting Miss Anthony to make us a visit. She has had a very remarkable dream. The physician ordered her from Philadelphia to Atlantic City for her health. While in the latter place, she had a very vivid dream one night. She thought she was being burnt alive in one of the hotels, and when she arose in the morning, told her niece what she had dreamed. "We must pack at once and go back to Philadelphia," she said. This was done, and the next day the hotel in which they had been and ten other hotels and miles of the boardwalk were destroyed by fire.

Unfortunately, in her haste to escape the holocaust, Miss Anthony had apparently neglected to inform the hotel clerk of her precognition.

Philosophers have often included consideration of the psychic in their reflections. Schopenhauer maintained that, from a philosophical point of view, psychic phenomena are most important aspects of human experience, that every scientist should feel obligated to know about them.

Immanuel Kant cleverly put his finger on the attitude of most people toward the subject. In his book *Dreams of a Spirit Seer*, in which he substantiated and validated Emanuel Swedenborg's incredible supernormal material, he stated:

> Philosophy . . . is often much embarrassed when she encounters on her march certain facts she dares not doubt, yet will not believe, for fear of ridicule. . . . This is the case with ghost stories. In short, there is no reproach to which philosophy is so sensitive as that of credulity, or the suspicion of any connection with vulgar superstitions. That is why ghost stories are always listened to and well-received in private, but pitilessly disavowed in public.

William James, as is well known, was a staunch advocate of extrasensory perception. This brilliant Harvard psychologist put his inquiring, original mind at the disposal of the S.P.R. for the two years he was president

*Andrew Lang, *Crystal Gazing.*

of the organization; and he was instrumental in the founding of the Boston S.P.R., which was a forerunner of the American Society. James took the long view, knowing that positive proof of the supernormal would be interminably delayed. He wrote: "It is my deeper belief that we psychic researchers have been too precipitate with our hopes; and that we must expect to mark progress not by quarter centuries but by half centuries or whole centuries."

Perhaps the interest Dr. Carl G. Jung had in psychic matters was enhanced by a ghost, although it undoubtedly began at home, where his mother was herself a very psychic person. In 1920 he visited at a country home rented by a friend, and during the nights he spent there he experienced various ghostly phenomena which gradually increased in strength. Jung says* that they included raps, unpleasant odors, a sound of rushing movements, and the dropping of liquid. One night (his last in the house, incidentally) he saw the head of a woman lying about sixteen inches away from him on his pillow. One of the eyes was wide open and staring at him.

Jung got up and lit a candle, and the head disappeared. Nevertheless, the famous psychologist spent the rest of the night sitting up in a chair.

Sigmund Freud, incidentally, was a member of both the English and American Societies for Psychical Research. He once wrote to Hereward Carrington, "If I had my life to live over again, I should devote myself to psychical research rather than to psychoanalysis."

When *Man the Unknown* appeared, Dr. Alexis Carrel told of the cures he had witnessed at Lourdes and made the startling declaration that "clairvoyance and telepathy are a primary datum of scientific observation." A Nobel prize winner in physiology and medicine, Dr. Carrel was nonetheless subjected to a whirlwind of ridicule and scorn for such statements.

Spuk by Fanny Moser, Baden bei Zurich, 1950.

Sir William Crookes, one of England's greatest physicists, also reaped the whirlwind for his staunch defense of his experiments with the materialization of spirits. But he never retracted his statements that he was convinced of the reality of the wonders he had seen.

At the time of his death Thomas Alva Edison was trying to invent a machine which would facilitate communication with the departed. And Abraham Lincoln during his lifetime was a very psychic person who saw omens in dreams. He even had a dream which predicted his own violent death.

Under the date of April 23, 1863, the *Chicago Tribune* ran an item telling about a spiritual soiree Abraham Lincoln, the President of the United States, held in the Crimson Room at the White House for the purpose of testing the alleged supernatural powers of medium Charles E. Shockle. For some half an hour various phenomena were seen, raps were heard, tables moved. The picture of Henry Clay which hung on the wall was swayed more than a foot, and two candelabra, which had been presented to President Adams by the Bey of Algiers, with no such intent in mind, were twice raised near to the ceiling.

Lincoln is now purported to haunt the White House, whenever he has time from his other etheric duties, which are enormous according to Spiritualists.

Mme. Frances Alda is another busy ghost, continuing her interest in music by being the haunt in residence at the Metropolitan Opera House. The shade of Mme. Alda is purported to rustle into a performance in a noisy taffeta dress, thrash about in her seat, crumple and crinkle her program, with the evident intent to make as much commotion as possible while the soprano on stage is singing. She hisses, "Flat! flat!" and nudges whoever happens to be her unfortunate neighbor. (One such operagoer swears her ribs were black and blue from the jabbings.) Since this behavior is typical of the lady after she had retired from

131

her own singing career, those who knew her give her full credit now. But the ghost of Mme. Alda always disappears before she can be held accountable.

David Belasco, theatrical producer and dramatist of the early decades of this century, issued a booklet with the same title as his highly popular play *The Return of Peter Grimm*. In it was the following statement:

> My mother convinced me that the dead come back by coming to me at the time of her death. One night . . . I was awakened . . . and was then greatly startled to see my dear mother (whom I knew to be in San Francisco) standing close by me. As I strove to speak and to sit up she smiled at me a loving, reassuring smile, spoke my name—the name she called me in my boyhood—"Davy, Davy, Davy," then, leaning down seemed to kiss me; then drew away a little and said, "Do not grieve. All is well and I am happy"; then moved towards the door and vanished.
>
> The next day I related the incident to my family and expressed the conviction that my mother was dead.

Later he received a telegram to the effect that his mother had died the night before, just about the time he had seen her. He concludes:

> I am aware that such experiences as this are, by some, explained on a theory of what they call "thought transference," but such explanation, to me, is totally inadequate. I am sure that I did see her. And other experiences of a kindred nature served to confirm my knowledge that what we call supernatural is, after all, at most but supernormal. Then, after long brooding on the subject, I determined to write a play, in terms of what I conceived to be actuality, dealing with the return of the dead.

Broadway columnist Danton Walker of the *New York Daily News* had a hobby of collecting ghost stories from the famous personalities he knew, his own interest stemming from the tales told him by his childhood nurse and augmented by a ghost which haunted his house. In 1956, a few years before his death, Walker published *Spooks Deluxe** in which, among others, he tells Ida Lupino's strange telephone adventure.

*Franklin Watts, Inc., New York.

The dramatic actress wrote that her story involved a close friend of her father's whom she gave the fictitious name of Andrew Meyer. She was very fond of him, as was the rest of her family, and he was a frequent visitor at their home. At the time of which she wrote Miss Lupino was about nine years old. She and her mother, Connie, and her father, Stanley, were living at the home of her grandmother on the outskirts of London. One night about half past ten she was still awake when the telephone rang. She says:

I went to the phone, took the receiver off the hook and heard a faint voice on the line. Finally, the voice became stronger and I could understand the message, repeated monotonously several times, "I must talk to Stanley. It is terribly important."

I answered, "Oh, it's you, Uncle Andy! Daddy isn't home yet." But the voice kept repeating the same words, and this time quite distinctly, "Stanley—I must talk to Stanley—it's terribly important."

I asked him to hold the line until I could get Granny. She went to the phone and I heard her say, "Why, Andy—are you ill? I'll ask Stanley to call you the moment he comes in." Then the phone was cut off and there was no further talk. . . .

About half an hour later, Stanley and Connie arrived home and I gave Stanley Uncle Andy's message. Connie dropped suddenly into a chair and looked as though she were going to faint.

Stanley said I must be mistaken—and, anyway, it was time for me to be in bed.

Granny said, "But she's *not* mistaken, Stanley, and I think you had better call Andy. He sounded as though he was very ill."

"Mom—," Stanley answered, and I'll never forget how tense his voice sounded, "Andrew Meyer is dead. He hung himself three days ago."

If Charles Darwin hadn't published *The Origin of Species* when he did, Alfred Russel Wallace would probably have received credit for the discovery of the law of natural selection, for this naturalist had come upon the same theory independently at the same time that Darwin did. Wallace was in later years a strong believer in the reality of communication with spirits, and he spent his time trying scientifically to account for the phenomena he had witnessed. On a lecture tour of the United States Wallace was the house guest in California of Senator and Mrs. Leland Stanford, who had recently lost their son. They both assured him that they had had long-continued communication through several different mediums with their son, and under circumstances that "rendered doubt impossible."

It is understood that Stanford left considerable money to be used for psychical research at the college he founded at Palo Alto, California. Whether plans are in process for its use for this purpose cannot be ascertained. If Stanford University does not have a seat of parapsychology, however, there is a growing list of institutions of higher education which do devote special attention to the subject.

Besides Duke University, there are in the United States St. Joseph's College in Philadelphia, City College in New York, St. John's University at Jamaica, New York, and San Diego College in California. In Canada, the subject is followed at the University of Saskatchewan and at McGill University at Montreal. The University of Utrecht in Belgium and the University of Frieburg in Germany have departments where research in this field is carried on. Individual researchers in parapsychology are also active at the University of Virginia and the University of Colorado.

It might surprise many to know that in the Department of Physiology at the University of Leningrad in the U.S.S.R. extensive researches are being conducted in telepathy. There are other countries behind the Iron Curtain where ESP investigations are going on, among them Czechoslovakia and Poland. Parapsychological studies have not only become almost a matter of course on the general academic scene of the world, but the list of countries which now have their own societies for psychical research is imposing: Argentina, Austria, Belgium, Denmark, England, Finland, France, Germany, Greece, India, Italy, Mexico, Netherlands, Norway, Sweden, Switzerland, Union of South Africa, Uruguay, and the United States.

We can leave it to the Roman orator Cicero to sum up the arguments as put forth by the famous, and the curious around the world:

> What we have to do with is the facts, since of the cause we know little. Neither are we to repudiate these phenomena, because we sometimes find them imperfect, or even false, any more than we are to distrust that the human eye sees, although some do this very imperfectly, or not at all.

ESP's Twin Sister

ESP HAS A SIAMESE twin, psychokinesis, known by her handy initials—PK. PK, defined as the exercise of direct mental influence over a physical object or an objective process, is so closely interrelated with extrasensory perception that the two are often distinguished only with pedantic exactitude. The idea of "mind over matter" has been part of the history of the world, just as mind reading has, and prophecy. It is only very recently, however, that it has been tested in a laboratory.

As Dr. Rhine has said,* "The hypothesis that mind can directly influence matter has no standing whatever in the scientific world, but neither had precognition. The one was hardly more difficult to accept than the other." But because one day a gambler walked into the Duke Parapsychology Laboratory with a firm conviction that when he was "hot' the dice would fall for him the way he willed them to, a whole new series of experiments got under way. Now a long existing but unexplained phenomenon of psychical research is beginning to knuckle under to the exploratory tactics of laboratory experiment.

Without scientific sanction, psychokinesis had long been reported to exist in terms of some unknown psychic power and many thoughtful people had taken it seriously. They knew that at least some of the carefully investigated hauntings, poltergeists, faith-healing, and mediumship phenomena must have some basis in fact, and so they gave them the courtesy of their attention.

Of haunted houses, Dr. Rhine says that "The occurrence

*The Reach of the Mind.

of unexplainable effects associated with a particular house has been reported time and again throughout the ages. After studying many accounts of these hauntings, involving ghostly touches, noises, doors left ajar, sometimes with apparitions experienced even by children, and—judging by their behavior—by pet animals, the scientist may well find himself unable to believe or yet to reject them in their totality. Sometimes the evidence is such as to pass all requirements except that of experiment, and yet its very incredibility demands something more, and judgment must be suspended."

The fantastic performances of what is still called by its German name of "poltergeist" or "noisy ghost" warrants presentation in detail. No Johnny-come-lately, but an anomaly through the ages, this obstreperous practical joker recently made the entire American public temporarily poltergeist conscious through the medium of an alert and ubiquitous press. In 1958, in Seaford, Long Island, the modest home of Mr. and Mrs. James M. Herrmann was turned into a shambles. Bottles suddenly blew their tops and sugar bowls went into orbit. A bookcase was turned over when no one was near it. A seventeen pound portable phonograph was hurled across the room—by nobody visible. Other treasured possessions were knocked down or thrown about, and a flask of holy water was most disrespectfully treated.

Nationwide publicity resulted in numerous newspaper and magazine interviews and television appearances for the Herrmann family. They no doubt enjoyed the notoriety and the excitement that had come into their hitherto quiet lives but relished the eventual cessation of the shenanigans still more. A good time was had by all, several penetrating opinions were given by eminent authorities, but no one got a picture of the *geist* in action. No one ever does.

Shortly before the Herrmanns started dodging, the

James Mikulecky home in Rest Haven, Illinois suffered similar clownish indignities, less exploited by the fourth estate. Chairs raised themselves halfway to the ceiling; magazines sailed about; a stuffed kitten jumped off the TV set; cabbages and tomatoes chased indiscriminately about the kitchen.

In July, 1957 in Hartville, Missouri, much consternation was aroused when little Betty Jane Ward, aged nine, won the attention of a poltergeist who didn't like grocery stores. Whenever Betty Jane went shopping with her mother, all the goods flew off the shelves and counters. At home she had to put up with a pail of water tipping itself over, and soap which wouldn't stay in the soap dish.

While these are recent and circumscribed, the records are full of psychokinetic activity from long ago and far away. In 1810 coffins were disturbed in closed vaults in Stanton, Suffolk, England; in 1922 in Chico, California rocks fell straight down from the sky over the area of one city block and in no other spot. As early as 355 A.D. at Bingem-am-Rhine, Germany, stones were thrown, people pulled out of bed, raps and terrific blows reported. In 530 Deacon Helpidius, physician to King Theodoric, son of Clovis, suffered a "diabolical infestation," particularly showers of stones which occurred within his home. In 1853 a small house belonging to the Residency of Cheribon, Java was besieged by invisible pranksters; and in Clayton, California in 1958 household utensils flew about for over two weeks in the home of oil worker Anthony Gomez. As recently as March 15, 1962 the Associated Press reported activity in Indianapolis, Indiana as follows: "The glassware has quit flying around and breaking objects at Mrs. Renate Beck's house—which could indicate that Henry the Poltergeist has departed or has lost his psychokinetic power."

Psychokinetic power is the definition of poltergeist activity now currently popular. And it is certainly the one

138

that the Duke Laboratory underwrites. But many other theories have been advanced, varying from the literal translation of the spiritists, who say it is actually a mischievous ghost, to those realists who suspect the energy of magnetic fields, seismological disturbances or underground water streams setting up subsonic vibrations. The "I wouldn't believe it if I saw it" people fall back as always on mass hysteria or collective hallucination, or even mass hypnotism.

The fact that poltergeists are so frequently associated with children affords ground for the favorite hypothesis —that all the odd happenings are being produced by the child. It is true that with the commotion in full spate, a son or daughter of the house has been caught tossing a dish or pushing over a china closet to increase and prolong the delicious excitement and attention. But the idea of the child being the sole instigator does not hold too much water. Usually the disturbances are too continuous and too vigorous for the lone efforts of the most ambitious adolescent prankster; and they often occur where no child is at hand to blame.

For that matter, poltergeisting offers adults a splendid field for innocent and hearty fun. A gentleman of Windsor, Nova Scotia, who shall be nameless because he was the judge of the County Probate Court, wrote to the American Society for Psychical Research for help in 1906, saying that he and several other reliable witnesses had seen vegetables and coins flying about, barrels rolling down the streets, and the figure of a headless man several times in the cellar. Investigators discovered a group of young men in the village who had conspired to give the old party a rough time. But that's beside the point. Enough manifestations have occurred in which no fraud was ever discovered, or even indicated.

In many well-reported cases the manifestations produced have been those which no human being could duplicate, even with all the means of modern science at his disposal. There have been reports of lighted matches dropping from the ceiling, objets d'art falling from great heights without being damaged, and unbreakable stone paperweights shattering. Sometimes a fragile vase has been safely hurled with intense force, and the next moment an anvil has floated leisurely by. Rocks arrive through the walls or roofs, usually hot to the touch, yet people hit with them may not be harmed. While in flight objects are said to be able to negotiate corners, stop and back up, or turn around.

Frequently the nature and variety of the activity seems to indicate a definite intelligence at work, although, to be sure, an invisible intelligence. One of the best documented instances of organized persecution was inflicted upon Presbyterian minister Eliakim Phelps and his family in Stratford, Connecticut in 1850. As reported in the *New Haven Journal and Courier,* the actions occurred with extreme force at frequent intervals over a period of about eighteen months. The first signs of the poltergeist greeted the family when they returned from church one Sunday to find the furniture strewn about, and in one room eleven curious and extremely life-like figures constructed of clothing, arranged in a tableau depicting a scene of worship.

From this time on the rooms were closely attended, yet tableaux appeared when the Reverend Phelps was positive no human being could have entered the room. Clothing was somehow gathered from all parts of the house, in spite of the strict watch which was kept to see that nothing of the sort could possibly occur. Witnesses, according to the *New Haven Journal,* declared that in a short space of time so many figures were constructed that it would not have been possible for half a dozen persons working steadily for several hours, to have completed their design and arranged the picturesque scene. Yet these things happened with the whole house on the alert. One of the wierdest and most original manifestations in the Phelps home is said to have occurred before the eyes of the entire family, when the flower design in the rug suddenly stood upright and grew into a living plant, its leaves covered with strange hieroglyphics. It did so.

There are many other cases on record in which the poltergeist seemed to give evidence of human intelligence. In Ireland, in 1877, in the Derrygonnelly case, Sir William Barrett found a poltergeist who was able to show off his knowledge of arithmetic. Barrett first satisfied himself that the strange noises and rappings could not have been made by any of the inmates of the house, for they were all on view. Then he saw a stone "fall from the void." Barrett challenged the mysterious agent of the knockings to echo by raps the number he mentally indicated; which it did. Further, putting his hands into the side pockets of his overcoat, Professor Barrett asked that it knock a number corresponding to the number of fingers which he extended. The experiment was repeated four times, with varying numbers, and in each case the answer was given correctly.

Of his investigations of the Derrygonnelly case and other unusual occurrences of this nature Sir William said:

> When little boys throw stones into a pool, we do not seek for the meaning or purpose behind their activity; it is sufficient to assume that it affords them pleasure—and perhaps even greater pleasure if they find it irritates grown-ups! I do not know why we should imagine there are no fools or naughty children in the spirit world, possibly they are as numerous there as here.

So Barrett has brought us back to the children, only this time the theory is that they are invisible ones.

Another poltergeist explanation more closely related to PK is offered by Raynor C. Johnson of the University of Melbourne:

The entity involved is a mental fragment expressing a group of primitive ideas or actions, but associated with a bottled-up reservoir of emotional energy [and] when this energy is completely discharged, the "poltergeist" is no more.

Dr. Nandor Fodor, psychiatrist, adds to this that: "The human mind can be so split-off that part of it may function in apparent independence." And this is where the Herrmann's young Jimmie or little Mary Jane Ward come in. For, according to Fodor, it is the pubescent child's unresolved tensions of sexual stress which involuntarily produce the sudden surges of kinetic energy which cause the poltergeist manifestations.

Dr. J. Gaither Pratt of the Duke Parapsychological Laboratory visited the Herrmann family at the time of the activity of their spook, who did not choose to perform for him. He was quoted in the *New York Times* as saying that he has "never seen objects move as a result of mental power" but that experiments had been made at Duke which "lead to the definite conclusion that there is some sort of influence of mind over matter." Dr. Pratt particularly concentrated his attention during his visit on young Jimmie Herrmann, hoping to discover whether the boy's mind was unconsciously causing the objects around him to be so flighty.

When objects fly among primitive races it is usually attributed to the medicine men or witch doctors. Anthropologists with experience among the American Indians or the ethnological groups of the South Sea Islands and Africa frequently report performances that defy natural explanation. In religious ceremonies of these elementary peoples they have witnessed the levitation of objects, the hurling of stones by unseen hands, or what they were convinced was actual magical rain making. Anthropologist Geoffrey Gorer tells of timing a West African Negro who remained under water in full view for forty-five minutes. Buried alive under the traditional six feet of earth, Oriental fakirs claim to be able to exist for hours and even days. "Whether," Dr. Rhine writes, "they really do anything that cannot be explained by the physics of the body, we are unable to say as yet. But *if* they do, there is then so much more to be discovered about man that it will be apparent our academic sciences are only working in a fraction of their true domain . . ."

Dr. Rhine adds that, "Psychokinesis may already have slipped into medicine in disguise. At any rate in the new field called 'psychosomatic medicine' organic effects are casually enough attributed to the state of mind of the patient. It is still a question as to what goes on between the state of mind and the resultant change; but the close tie-up of the two as a causal unit in reproducing disease is now accepted medical knowledge. Only a generation ago all this was superstition to the orthodox physician . . . If there is PK in any one of these occurrences, the magnitude of its importance justifies any amount of patient and exhaustive investigation."

Naturalists and world travellers such as Ivan Sanderson occasionally return from remote spots with tall tales and unbelievable yarns. But Sanderson has authenticating papers signed by witnesses to verify the following, which seems to indicate psychokinesis in action in its most virulent form.

The incident occurred in Belize, British Honduras where a little Mexican conjurer had just arrived in town to entertain the native population. The local theatre was filled as he performed simple magical acts. A native Honduran in the audience began to heckle the performer and to shout that he was no good and anyone could do better. The Mexican stood it quietly for a while and then stopped the show and asked the man to shut up. The interruptions continued. Finally, the magician pointed his finger at the man and cried out, "Pain, get him." The heckler immediately doubled up in agony, writhing and screaming. "Have you had enough?" asked the Mexican. Then he said, "Pain, leave." The man was immediately relieved. But for some reason, possibly alcoholic, he was not satisfied, and soon again he began to shout and disturb the performance. This time the conjurer felt he had really had it. He pointed his finger at the interrupter once more and stared at him fixedly as he said one word, "Pain." This time the native fell to the floor screaming. But he was given no surcease, and so he was carried out into the lobby of the theatre. Every doctor present rushed out, feeling fortunate to have the opportunity to examine him. Ivan Sanderson also saw him there, as did Dr. Rex Cheverton, Senior Medical Officer in British Honduras, and later Senior Officer for the entire British Medical Colonial Service. Sanderson describes the native's appearance as being pale, cheesy looking, and anguished. The sick man gripped his abdomen and cried that it felt as if something were eating him. The doctors inspected him and saw that the abdomen was sunken and pulled in as though a hand inside was gripping the flesh and squeezing it into a knot.

Dr. Cheverton quietly sent word into the auditorium for the magician to remove the "spell"; and the doctors watched the victim, who did not know this. But when inside the theatre the Mexican said, "Pain, leave," at that moment the man lying on the floor of the lobby let out his breath with a sigh, and his abdomen was observed to return to normal.

Not only can the mind inflict illness, it can also cure. The belief in the efficacy of faith healing, the laying on of hands, fetishes and charms, and objects which have been blessed or handled by some divine personage, is a concept lost in antiquity. But it was not until recently that the influence of the mind in this connection has been recognized.

In 1903 F.W.H. Myers spoke of the miracles of Lourdes

and the cures effected by Christian Science as "schemes of self-suggestion." He says that the suggestion of the curative power of the Lourdes water, for instance, is given out partly in books, partly by word of mouth, "and a certain percentage of persons succeed in so persuading themselves of that curative efficacy that when they bathe in the water they are actually cured."

Psychokinesis is again held accountable for the odd powers of the physical medium. The world-famous psychiatrist Carl Jung once wrote to Rhine of strange physical phenomena that had happened in his home just as he was about to begin to make a study of a medium located a few miles away. One of these consisted of the splitting of a very old, well-seasoned table top, accompanied by a pistol-like report. No one was near the table at the time.

Since wood is subject to splitting from natural causes, Dr. Rhine was forced to conclude about this that while very unusual, it was not impossible. But when he read in the psychiatrist's letter "that an old, steel bladed bread knife also went to pieces about the same time, accompanied by a similar loud explosive report," he says, "I was frankly puzzled. I have a photograph of the knife, which showed the blade clearly broken into four sections. The phenomenon still appears unexplainable to me in terms of anything known at present. The psychiatrist himself regards these happenings as cases of PK, in some way connected with the medium, although he does not pretend to know how the effects were produced."

Psychokinetic activity in relation to physical mediumship will be discussed more fully in a later chapter. No great amount of experimentation has been done with physical mediums, however; at least not nearly enough to suit Dr. Rhine.

"One could wish," he sighs, "for more studies like that of the English medium Stella C. by Harry Price, in the course of which large, automatically recorded drops in room temperature—as great as 11 degrees Fahrenheit—were obtained."

Another noteworthy investigation Rhine refers to was carried out by the two Drs. Osty, father and son, at the Institut Métapsychique in Paris. In this series of tests the Austrian medium, Rudi Schneider, was controlled by a screen of infrared radiation designed to record automatically any possible fraudulent move he might make. Effects were nevertheless obtained that challenged the limitations of the scientists' knowledge.

The basic need in all this investigation is, of course, experiment. Fortunately for the problem of testing PK, many people firmly believe that if they can't persuade race horses to win, at least they can mentally influence dice. This attribute was called to the attention of the Duke Laboratory by the young galloping domino specialist who visited it to discuss what he considered to be the role of ESP in social games of chance. "He also," says Dr. Rhine, "asserted stoutly his confident belief that he could mentally influence the fall of dice under the right conditions and accepted the challenge to demonstrate the point. He succeeded well enough to justify a thorough test of his claim."

Dr. Rhine was delighted to discover that the dice-throwing procedure was ideal for a laboratory test of the PK hypothesis. The various experimental controls could be applied to it, and it was a test which would appeal to and challenge the subjects. The records could be scored easily, and the average score to be expected from chance alone could be readily computed. It had everything. One of its great virtues was that everyone was able to throw dice. No special individuals had to be sought out as mediums. Dr. Rhine, his wife, their family members, friends, students, and even casual visitors all participated with enthusiasm. "It became a game with a serious justification," he says, "a social pastime that had full intellectual license. It lent itself to scientific control without unwarranted concessions to the subject's whims or beliefs. It was not hard for the subject to get the feeling that he *could* influence the dice; he could usually watch the results as he went along, and doing so added much to his interest."

A typical PK test run went as follows: With sevens as the target chosen for the runs, the subject was asked to shake a pair of dice in a cup and throw them onto a padded table top. Two sevens were, on the average, to be expected from pure chance in a run of twelve throws. But from the very beginning the PK scores tended to be above chance. There were never any strikingly high scores, none that were nearly as high as many of the ESP scores had been; but, on the other hand, more people were moderately successful with the dice throwing tests.

To indicate how closely spontaneous PK ties in with general extrasensory perception, here is the experience of a young woman named Irene, who told me her story personally. One morning while she was sleeping her roommate went out to the store. Returning with a heavy bag of groceries, the roommate considered pushing their bell button in the lobby of the apartment building, so Irene would have the door open for her when she arrived upstairs. She thought of this as she passed the intercom panel, and as she opened the downstairs door. She even looked back over her shoulder, thinking, "Maybe I should ring after all." But she didn't. While this was going on downstairs, in their apartment Irene heard the bell peal so loudly that she leaped out of bed and ran to the door.

Now does this indicate that the roommate's mind actually rang the bell by PK? Or did Irene get the message telepathically from her friend and then have an auditory hallucination that the bell was ringing? Not many parapsychologists would state that they knew exactly what happened. But something did. Something strange is certainly involved when psychokinesis is indicated. The implications are tremendous, but its practical application is still to be determined—possibly far, far in the future.

Whether PK as we find it at present sounds sufficiently encouraging to suggest a profitable trip to Las Vegas, the reader must decide for himself. The writer assumes no responsibility.

12 *The Problems of Mediumship*

mediumship have been a Herculean challenge to parapsychologists. But what is a scientist going to do when he sees, as did Sir William Crookes, a beautifully formed small hand rise up from an opening in a dining room table and give him a flower? Crookes had satisfied himself thoroughly that there was neither person nor paraphernalia under the table. He was himself holding the medium's hands and had his feet across her feet. There was even plenty of light and he could see everything that was going on. If this had been the only time such unusual manifestation presented itself to Crookes, he still might have doubted the testimony of his own senses; but similar and even much more astounding materializations were seen by him when several other persons were present and where precautions were stringent.

Investigators know that too many materializations are fraudulent. They are aware that some mediums can on occasion produce fine evidence that is apparently authentic, and then another time rig the proceedings with clever deceptions. This is curious, but it can be explained in most cases as due to the peculiar pressures of mediumship. A person making his living by his psychic powers frequently feels obliged to produce for his paying customers, even when he is not functioning at his best. Unfortunately, such powers are all too often sporadic.

Another aspect to be considered is the one brought out by Louis K. Anspacher in *Challenge of the Unknown*. "All psychic power," he says, "of whatsoever nature it may be, is a manifestation of the unconscious mind . . .

149

And the conscious mind does not avail us much in psychics. [Thus] the uneducated person may be the better fitted to be a [channel] for these recondite and mysterious unknown powers, for the simple reason that education sometimes gets in the way. Jeanne d'Arc was a peasant girl. Eusapia Palladino had very little education. Mrs. Piper, the most powerful mediumistic personality developed here in America, whose psychic manifestations were never diluted or compromised with fraud, was a very good and estimable woman of fine character; yet she had very little formal or intellectual education. Her psychic faculty . . . functioned most successfully in a state of trance when her conscious faculties were completely in abeyance."

Thus we can see why mediums are frequently tricky, according to Anspacher. "In their psychic state they relapse into that primal, puckish, jungle mind, the shrewd, instinctive, animal mind." Accordingly, in all psychic investigation with mediums, researchers do their best to establish rigid controls. The important mediums, like Mrs. Piper, seem to know that their unconscious is not to be completely trusted, and so they always insist upon the strictest test conditions.

Eusapia Palladino was a perfect example of the unreliable medium. This earthy Italian sensitive was undoubtedly the most exasperating with which psychical researchers ever had to deal. Wilfully practicing fraud wherever she thought she could get away with it, she preferred to put on an act for the eagerly credulous, avoiding with peasant guile the demands of a true trance state and conserving her paranormal powers. In most cases those who caught her in trickery publicized it until it was believed by the general public that all her manifestations had been exposed.

But this was far from the case. During the course of some twenty-five years she gave hundreds of seances to scientific groups all over Europe and many more hundreds to interested investigators, and at these she produced great quantities of physical phenomena which were never in any way proved to be fraudulent. The scientists imposed conditions such as would have made it impossible for her to use trickery, and still things occurred which were unbelievable. When deception was impossible, she came up with magnificent phenomena. As Hereward Carrington says in *The American Seances with Eusapia Palladino*,* "The facts, it is true are surprising; they are contrary to ordinary human experience, and on that account hard to believe. Even if one accepts them at the time of their occurrence, one is apt to lapse into skepticism a few days after witnessing the phenomena. The tendency is to believe that one *must* have been mistaken!" And yet Carrington was perfectly convinced that at a really *good* seance no trickery was used by Palladino and the phenomena were 100% genuine. Carrington concluded his book with: "I will only repeat once again my personal conviction, which remains unshaken after more than forty years, and despite all adverse criticism, viz., that we repeatedly witnessed, in Eusapia Palladino's seances, genuine physical phenomena of an extraordinary character which (if duly appreciated) would throw an entirely new light upon biology, psychology, and the whole structure of mechanistic science."

Carrington, an American who had devoted himself to exposing fraudulent mediums and knew all the tricks and how to contain them, was one of three staunch and highly qualified investigators, competent to deal with Eusapia's stratagems, who had tested her for the Society for Psychical Research. The other two trained observers were W. W. Baggally and Everard Feilding, neither of whom, when they started, believed in the genuineness of any paranormal physical manifestations whatsoever. Carrington and Bag-

*Garrett Publications, New York, 1954.

gally were both accomplished amateur magicians, who felt that they could be sure to catch Palladino if she attempted any jiggery-pokery.

These three gentlemen, chaperoned by their secretary, isolated themselves with Palladino in the Hotel Victoria in Naples during much of November and December, 1908. There they held a series of seances where the strictest possible controls were always observed. A cabinet was arranged across one corner of the room and behind it was a small tea table on which were placed various light toys, which Eusapia had not seen. She sat outside the cabinet with her back to it beside a small oblong table. One man sat on each side of her, holding her hands and controlling her feet with their legs and feet. Sometimes a third was under the table holding her feet with his hands. There was always light in the room.

Feilding reported in the *Proceedings* S.P.R.:

The phenomena included levitations of the table at which we sat. As a rule the table began to rock in a manner explainable by the ordinary pressure of her hands. It then tilted in a manner not so explainable, and finally it would leave the ground entirely and rise to a height of a foot or two rapidly, remain there an appreciable time and then come down. . . . No precautions that we took hindered in the slightest. She had no hooks, and we could never discern the slightest movement of her knees or feet. Sometimes a partial levitation or tilt would last a very long time, even a minute. We would press it down and it would come up again as though suspended on elastics. . . . We were constantly touched on the arm, shoulder or head by something which we could not see. The next development was grasps through the curtain by hands, living hands with fingers and nails. This occurred at times when we were absolutely certain that Eusapia's own hands were separately held on the table in front of her. These grasps, if fraudulent, could only have been done by an accomplice behind the curtain. There was no accomplice behind the curtain.

Next these hands became visible, generally between the parting of the curtains over Eusapia's head. Once a hand came out from the side, not the middle of the curtain, seized Mr. Baggally and almost upset him off his chair.

Often there were violent noises inside the cabinet, as though the tea table were being shaken. It then itself appeared over Eusapia's shoulder and landed on our table horizontally with its top resting on our table and its legs pointing into the cabinet. It would appear to hang there and try to climb on our table, which it never succeeded in doing. . . . The flageolet tapped me on the head, the tambourine jumped on my lap, the tea-bell was rung and presently appeared, ringing, over Eusapia's head, carried by a hand which attached it quickly to her hair, reappeared, detached the bell itself, rang it again over Eusapia's head and threw it on to the seance table. . . . During this time the light was sufficient for the shorthand writer from his table eight or nine feet from Eusapia to see the hand which carried the bell.

Now, did Eusapia Palladina mass-hypnotize these three S. P. R. investigators and their secretary day after day into "seeing things" that weren't there? Did she command the attention of some of the most brilliant men in Europe over a period of twenty-five years by the stock in trade of the stage illusionist? Did she have the help of "spirits?" Or could she exert some kind of mental energy of a psychokinetic nature as yet little understood? These are questions perhaps to be answered when another psychic of her stature appears who will be observed and checked with modern equipment.

This may not be as soon as could be hoped. Whether it is because of the mental climate in which we live, where mediums are made fun of and in some areas considered illegal, or whether for some other reason, physical mediums are becoming even less prevalent.

The few great ones who *have* existed have never cared much about allowing parapsychologists to study them. Being analyzed and prodded with scientific zeal doesn't seem to appeal to them. Can we really blame them? Scientific investigation of physical mediumship is one of the greatest invasions of personal privacy imaginable.

Mental mediums can be tested, and are tested, without

recourse to such extreme measures. Many mental mediums have passed rigorous investigations of their integrity with flying colors, for all that is needed is to hire a detective to shadow them and all their contacts (as was done with Mrs. Leonard and Mrs. Piper) to learn that they are not gaining information about their sitters from outside sources. There are many questions as to where their insight into the personal lives of the sitter and his family and friends, living and dead, is coming from: Is it telepathy from the sitter or from some other person? Is it a sort of clairvoyant retrocognition or supernormal knowledge of the past life of someone who previously lived? Is it from the spirit world, as the sensitive herself usually claims? Though the answer may be in doubt, the honesty of the medium can usually be ascertained with almost complete certainty.

In more cases than not the sensitive is a minister of a Spiritualist Church. She has undergone years of training in a class, sitting with another medium for the development of her psychic powers. She has now reached a position where she commands the respect and homage of her followers.

She usually believes that she is an intermediary between two worlds and that she receives her powers from spirits who are trying to prove their continued existence through her. She is sure that she has an etheric guide who gives her assistance. Her congregation eagerly accepts her as a chosen emissary to make contact between those who have passed on and those who have not. She believes that her work is most valuable and important.

The modern scientist, however, does not consider her as a religious personality at all. He defines a medium as an individual in whose presence paranormal phenomena occur at times, and on whose presence their occurrence is somehow dependent. The scientist views the medium with the same impartial eye with which he observes an amoeba under his microscope. In view of this objectivity, it is amusing that so many persons think of psychical researchers as fuddy-duddy old parties out to prove survival. They are more likely to be vigorous young or middle-aged men inquisitive about the unusual phenomena of psi. In fact, if they have any preconceived convictions to begin with, more of them probably believe that all this "spiritist nonsense is mere flapdoodle."

When the parapsychologist undertakes the investigation of a physical medium it is no cursory affair. Initially, when the medium enters the laboratory, she undresses and is examined by doctors. Even the most intimate parts of her anatomy will be inspected to make sure that she has concealed nothing. She may be asked to swallow repulsive potions to blanket anything she might have hidden in her esophagus with the intent of regurgitating it as "ectoplasm" during the seance.* Her hair is carefully examined to make sure she has nothing hidden in it. Then she is sewed into a tight-fitting one-piece garment.

The psychic is next taken to a simple, sparsely furnished room where she has never been before and seated beside men and women who are strangers to her. If she asks permission to work in a cabinet or closed space (which she believes allows spirit forces better to accumulate their power for action), she is provided with a curtained-off cubicle in a corner. But, although she is allowed to sit in this, her hands and feet must stick out of the curtains and be controlled so that she can't secretly use them to propel objects. So two members of the circle which is investigating her hold her hands and feet carefully during the entire performance.

Nowadays, there will be movie cameras, tape recorders and infra-red film from which the dark holds no

---

*Ectoplasm is the substance of which materializations are composed. It is capable of taking on various shapes and of exerting or conveying force. It is claimed that fraudulent mediums may swallow gauze or other substances and regurgitate them to simulate this ectoplasm.

secrets. The fact that the medium may insist on sitting without light might be questioned by some, even though she explains that spirit forces have more power in the dark. Unfortunately, so does trickery.

Now, tests such as these may go on for days or weeks, or even months, as they did with the medium Eva C., who was examined in just this manner for years by Drs. A. von Schrenck-Notzing and Gustave Geley, with extremely controversial results. Eva C. was also examined by the Society for Psychical Research, and the outcome was termed inconclusive, although she produced implausible phenomena under highly controlled conditions.

So, with the unenticing prospect of tests such as this, can anyone wonder that mediums do not very often offer their services to science? What will science do for them? They do not need to prove their powers to themselves or their followers, and they have already learned that all the proof they can offer won't convince anyone who doesn't want to be convinced. If nothing occurs of interest at a scientific seance in which the medium is carefully controlled, it will probably be assumed that it was because she *was* controlled that she could do nothing. Instead, she may have been nervous, ill at ease, uncomfortable, tense, and possibly feeling antagonism from some members of her audience.

Then we also have the fact that if phenomena *are* produced at such a seance, if with all these stringent conditions, unexplained materializations or activities *do* occur, they will be cried down by a great many who read the published reports about them. "These things are preposterous," it will be protested. "They just don't happen."

We haven't mentioned this same professional medium, or her sister sensitive whose manifestations are of the mental variety, as she might sit for card-guessing experiments of the type used at Duke University. Perhaps it is just as well. Despite possible initial success, fatigue at the endless repetition would soon be all too apparent.

So this is very likely why there is so little actual scientific proof of mediumship. The entire subject is just too complicated, too highly involved, for proof ever to come easily.

And yet the evidence of the authenticity of some physical mediums, despite all this, is surprisingly good. Daniel Dunglas Home, a Scottish psychic, was one who produced much that was so startling it has aroused controversy ever since. Several persons with the authority of their professions and their high reputations behind them, absolutely swore that they had seen things done by Home that can't be done. Two of the foremost scientists of the period, Sir William Crookes, inventor of the X-Ray tube, and Dr. Robert Hare, declared his phenomena to be genuine; but they could not interest other scientists to come and observe him, for the claims made for him were more than could possibly be accepted. Over fifty witnesses, however, have testified to the authenticity of such feats as the following: Home put his face into a fire of hot coals and was not burned. He rose in the air frequently—on one occasion in front of three people, Lords Lindsay and Adare and Captain Wynne, he floated out of a window and back in at another window. A small accordion occasionally played by itself in Home's presence.

Sir William Crookes made a wire cage in which he placed the instrument, so that no human hands could touch it, and it continued to play merrily. We are not dependent upon Crookes' testimony alone for knowledge of Home's manifestations. Others have written about it as well. But because *Lady* Crookes' statement of what she saw is so graphic, let's keep it in the family and quote her certified account: She says that she had seen Home walking about with the accordion and that then it "was immediately taken from his hand by a cloudy appearance, which soon seemed to condense into a distinct human form, clothed in a filmy drapery . . . The accordion began to play . . . and the figure gradually advanced towards me till it almost touched me, playing continuously. It was semi-transparent, and I could see the sitters through it all the time." Home remained across the room from this apparition.

The famous psychic brothers Willi and Rudi Schneider were studied carefully for years while performing feats no magician could possibly duplicate—at least not under the conditions imposed on them by the Schneider boys' investigators.

The well-known challenge which Houdini and other magicians have issued to mediums—that they could duplicate any feat the psychic might perform—has not been accepted for one specific reason. Houdini was answered, "We will accept your challenge if you will produce these phenomena under the very same conditions that we do, with no magical properties of any sort." This Houdini was not willing nor able to undertake.

There has been much controversy about the message which Houdini was supposed to try to send back to his wife after his death. Did he or did he not get it through to her? Mental medium Arthur Ford in 1929 handed Beatrice Houdini a list of words and her pet name, "Rosabelle," which was the key to the secret cipher the Houdinis had used in their mind reading act. He said that he had received this through his spirit control Fletcher. Mrs. Houdini wrote a public letter confirming the fact that this was the code her deceased husband had intended to convey through a medium if he were able. Her letter was published in Walter Winchell's column. She said she was satisfied that her husband had communicated with her. At a later date Mrs. Houdini rescinded this statement, possibly fearing that she had indicated too much naivéte and credulity in accepting the message as genuine.

Perhaps the medium with the best standing in scientific circles in America is Mrs. Eileen J. Garrett, president of the Parapsychology Foundation. For years she has not given readings to the general public but has saved all her time and talents for controlled investigation by researchers. Her urge is strong to learn what causes her unusual capabilities and how they can be used to the best advantage.

England has produced more outstanding mediums than any other country. The greatest of these is Mrs. Gladys Osborne Leonard, who held sittings for members of the Society for Psychical Research under test conditions for over fifty years. A tremendous amount of highly evidential material was produced through the activities of Mrs. Leonard's spirit control Feda, who was as real a personality to the thousands of Leonard-sitters as was the medium herself.

The Reverend Stainton Moses, an eminently respectable schoolmaster and minister of the gospel, for many years produced information which could have been acquired in no other way than supernormally.

To some people the evidence received through professional mediums is conclusive of survival of the human spirit. Dr. C. J. Ducasse, Professor Emeritus of Brown University, Providence, Rhode Island, and a former president of the American Philosophical Association, says in *A Critical Examination of the Belief in a Life After Death**:

> Except, perhaps, for a very few cases of "possession" . . . the most impressive sort of empirical evidence of survival is that provided by certain of the communications which are received through mediums or automatists, and which purport to emanate from particular deceased persons. . .
> That it is sometimes by no means easy to account for the content, the language, and the mannerisms of the communications otherwise than by the supposition that they really emanate

*Charles C. Thomas, Publisher, Springfield, Ill., 1961.

from the surviving spirits of the deceased will now be made evident by citation, even if only in summary form, of communications received by the late Professor J. H. Hyslop, purportedly from his deceased father, through the famous Boston medium, Mrs. Leonore Piper, who was studied by men of science probably for more years, and more systematically and minutely, than any other mental medium.

Dr. Hyslop went to Mrs. Piper as an anonymous sitter. His father was not a public character about whom she might have heard anything personal, having lived a very ordinary and retired life on his farm.

Mrs. Piper told Hyslop his name, James; his father's name, and the names of three others of his father's children. She also referred to a number of particular conversations the father had had with Professor Hyslop, to many special incidents and facts, and to family matters which she could have had no way of knowing by normal means. Many of the incidents mentioned were even unknown to Professor Hyslop himself, and were verified only by checking with other members of his family. He was told, for instance, that his father had trouble with his left eye, that he had a mark near his left ear, that he used to wear a thin coat or dressing gown mornings, and that at one time he wore a black skullcap at night; that he used to have one round and one square bottle on his desk and carried a brown-handled penknife with which he used to pare his nails; that he had a horse called Tom; that he used to write with quill pens which he trimmed himself; and so on. The communications also contained favorite pieces of advice, which were typical of the father, and these were worded in ways characteristic of his modes of speech. Professor Ducasse goes on:

> The question now arises, whether the imparting of such facts by a medium is explicable on some other hypothesis than that of communication with the deceased. Two other explanations—one normal and the other paranormal—suggest themselves. The first is, of course, that the medium obtained antecedently in some perfectly normal manner the information

communicated. One of the reasons why I chose Mrs. Piper's mediumship as example is that in her case this explanation is completely ruled out by the rigorous and elaborate precautions which were taken to exclude that possibility. For one thing, Dr. [Richard] Hodgson had both Mrs. Piper and her husband watched for weeks by detectives, to find out whether they went about making inquiries concerning the relatives and family history of persons they might have expected to come for sittings. Nothing in the slightest degree suspicious was ever found. Moreover, sitters were always introduced by Dr. Hodgson under assumed names. Sometimes, they did not come into the room until after Mrs. Piper was in trance, and then remained behind her where she could not have seen them even if her eyes had been open. . . . Many of the facts she gave out could not have been learned by a skilled detective [had she the means to employ one.] William James summed up the case against the fraud explanation in the statement that "not only has there not been one single suspicious circumstance remarked" during the many years in which she and her mode of life were under close observation, "but not one suggestion has ever been made from any quarter which might tend to explain how the medium, living the apparent life she leads, could possibly collect information about so many sitters by natural means."

Thus, because we do not merely believe but positively know that the information she gave was not obtained by her in any of the normal manners, there is in her case no escape from the fact that it had some paranormal source.

The paranormal explanation, according to Ducasse, alternative to the spiritist hypothesis is that, in the trance condition, Mrs. Piper, or her dissociated, secondary personalities, possess telepathic powers so extensive as to enable her to obtain the information she gives out from the minds of living persons who happen to have it; and this even if at the time it is buried in their subconsciousness, and no matter whether such persons be at the time with Mrs. Piper or anywhere else on earth. Or else that, in trance, Mrs. Piper has powers of retrocognitive clairvoyance so extensive as to enable her to observe the past life on earth of a deceased person.

But, Ducasse says further, besides the obscure true information provided by the medium, her dramatic presentation of the communicating spirits in their own personalities would call for extraordinary histrionic ability. How staggering a task this would be can only be appreciated by extensive perusal of the verbatim records of the conversations between sitter and communicators.

The Problems of Mediumship

As an illustration of evidence for true identity given through Mrs. Piper, the following highly abridged report of communications from the twin children, Margaret and Ruthie, of Dr. A. B. Thaw, is offered.*

Margaret had died at the age of six months and Ruthie at the age of fifteen months. Ruthie had begun to say a few words before she died. Phinuit, Mrs. Piper's control, at the first sitting mentioned trouble with teeth in connection with the children. . . . Margaret was teething when she died. Phinuit also said that one of the children wanted baby's beads. Margaret used to play with an older sister's bead necklace. Also referring to Margaret, Phinuit said that she had some flowers in her hand, that "she liked them and took them with her." Mrs. Thaw had placed three little flowers in Margaret's hand after her death.

Phinuit got much more in connection with Ruthie. Among the first things he mentioned was that she wanted to see the stars. For two or three months before her death Ruthie was fond of pointing at the stars through the window. At the beginning of the sitting Phinuit said she put her hand on Dr. Thaw's head, and afterwards wanted to pat his face, actions characteristic of the living Ruthie toward her father. Similarly she wanted to hear the "tick tick" in connection with her Uncle Alec, and it was he who chiefly used to hold his watch for her to hear. Another characteristic action was reproduced in connection with Mr. Melvin W. to whom Ruthie was said to want to wave her hand in a certain way. The living Ruthie had waved her hand in that manner to Mr. W. and to him only. Reference was made to her picture, and Mrs. Thaw was painting a picture of Ruthie when she was taken ill. The first time Mrs. Thaw wore fur at a sitting, the medium's hand stroked it, and Phinuit whispered "pussie" as Ruthie used to do.

Two or three times there seemed to be a direct control of the voice by Ruthie as if she were taking the place of Phinuit and speaking herself. She whispered *pttee* and *pussee* (pretty and pussie). The second occasion when Ruthie seemed to speak for herself was when Mrs. Piper had been asked to visit the Thaws in New York and they took her up the Hudson River to their country home. Dr. Hodgson, participating in a seance held there the first day, and taking notes of what was said, observed the medium's hand raised, turned somewhat diagonally with the forefinger pointing towards a picture on the far side of tions, *pttee, pttee*. The Thaws, who had been sitting with

*From Dr. Richard Hodgson's account in *Proceedings* S.P.R., Vol. xiii. pp. 384-5.

the room. At the same time she was saying, in Ruthie's inflec-bowed heads, did not see this gesture until their attention was drawn to it, and then they looked up and exclaimed over it. Later Dr. Thaw noted: "During the last month of Ruthie's life it was a regular morning custom to bring her to the room in which this sitting was held, and she would always point, as Mrs. Piper's hand had done, with *one* finger (unusual for a baby) and say *pt-tee, pt-tee*, just as in the sitting." This little habit had not been consciously in either the father or mother's mind since the baby's death six months before. Mrs. Piper had never been in the room until the actual time of the sitting. There were many other pictures in the room, but she pointed only to the one the baby had particularly loved.

Professor Hyslop himself, in concluding his discussion of Mrs. Piper's mediumship said: "When I look over the whole field of the phenomena and consider the supposi-tions that must be made to escape spiritism, which not only one aspect of the case but every incidental feature of it strengthened . . . I see no reason except the suspicions of my neighbors for withholding assent."

Yet, oddly enough, some mediums do not believe that they are transmitters of spirit messages. Eileen Garrett says frankly that she does not know where her power comes from, having no theory whether her alleged spirit controls are really discarnate entities, dissociated aspects of her own personality, or something else as yet unnamed.

Peter Hurkos has a similar outlook. The Dutch psychic first became aware of his extrasensory abilities after he was a grown man. He fell from a ladder and fractured his skull—a rather severe method of becoming sensitive and one not to be encouraged. From then on, he was able to read minds and locate lost articles and do other agile mental feats. During World War II he made himself gen-erally useful to the underground and afterwards to the police of France and Holland, helping to trace criminals.

Hurkos came to the United States to work with Dr. Andrija K. Puharich. Dr. Puharich tested him in a structure called a Faraday cage*, which appears to increase the sensitivity of mediums. Hurkos sat—very unwillingly—inside the cage and tried to identify the objects the doctor had on his desk outside. In the Faraday cage Hurkos was, according to Puharich, 80 per cent correct, and at times as much as 95 per cent.

The Dutch sensitive impressed Puharich with his other psychic talents as well. "The amazing thing about Peter," said Puharich, "is not so much that he has ESP—many people possess it—but that his percentage of accuracy is so high!"

Hurkos is active in a research foundation which has been organized with himself as the focal point. He is willing to be tested for science, he says; but he has no interest in founding a church, for he does not consider himself by any means to be a contact between worlds.

Edgar Cayce, the Virginia Beach seer, was a very religious Christian with fundamentalist leanings. For this reason he was very reluctant to develop his psychic powers and fought against it for many years. Finally he succumbed to the inevitable. He was eventually reconciled to it by the fact that he was able to help many people by the medical readings he gave when he was in a trance state. Cayce definitely did not believe in reincarnation; but when asleep he gave thousands of "life readings" which purported to be accounts of the previous lives of his sitters. Even when he was in the trance state, however, it was very seldom that anything was said which might indicate contact with the spirit world. The personality which spoke when Cayce was in trance claimed to be his own subconscious mind.

---

*Made of wire mesh and approximately eight feet square and eight feet high, it encloses a similar wooden compartment in which the subject sits alone. The outer wire compartment is then charged with 25,000 volts of electrical current supplied by a Van de Graef generator capable of producing 400,000 volts. Its basic principle is that of shielding—preventing electrical impulses from penetrating the walls to the subject. Other sensitives tested in the Faraday cage have also exhibited heightened powers.

Another psychic who does not think of himself as a medium is Ronald Edwin, who is called Mr. ESP. Edwin has admitted, in his book *Clock Without Hands,* that on occasion in the past when he was young and insecure, he did put on fraudulent mediumistic seances in England. But he denies utterly that he ever let any real spirits sneak into his routine. He is now a platform sensitive travelling in the Western Hemisphere, and he gives his audiences messages which are sometimes highly evidential.

"But," he says, "there's no evidence of any kind that my information comes from outside my own consciousness, or subconsciousness, or superconsciousness. And when I do get anything wrong I am not blaming the dead for it."

If spirits don't get the credit for mediumistic phenomena, then ESP certainly has to accept it. For the evidence strongly proves that something exists beyond explanation by any known law.

Dr. Rhine again, has this to say:

> The outcome of the scientific investigation of mediumship is best described as a draw. Hardly anyone would claim that all the investigations of seventy-five years or more have had the effect of *dis*proving the claim that if a man die he shall in some manner or other be capable of "living again." On the other hand, no serious scientific student of the field of investigation could say that a clear, defensible, scientific confirmation of the hypothesis has been reached.

Some of the leading scholars believed the hypothesis had been proved, he says, and "as many of equal qualifications were convinced, after examination of the evidence, of the inadequacy of the proof." Some, like William James and William McDougall, suspended judgment, but kept an open mind.

13 Psychedelics and Out-of-Body Experiences

WHEN AN OLD-FASH-
ioned witch rode around on a broomstick, she probably
thought she really did. But, as the story goes, before she
got off the ground she had to rub herself all over with
some sort of magic deep-penetrating beauty cream. Modern research would suggest that it was the cream which
gave her the idea she was starting for the moon.

Folklore, fairy tales, and legends hint that certain substances have been used from time immemorial to induce
supernormal states. Vision-producing substances, such as
are found in the peyote (a species of cactus) and in specific types of mushrooms, have been used for thousands
of years by the shamans, priests, or medicine men of
primitive religions. The *Amanita muscaria*—a mush-
room considered to have divine properties—was eaten
by the Mongols and the Egyptians, who used it to foretell
the future and project their minds into a metaphysical
world. Certain Mexicans still use the sacred mushrooms
in their religious ceremonies.

Among the Mixtecan Indians now living in Southern
Mexico, the local wise man displays remarkable powers
of clairvoyance after eating the sacred mushrooms. In
recent years, a scientific expedition to Mexico composed
of, among others, R. Gordon Wasson and his wife Dr.
Valentina P. Wasson, discovered that the shaman, after
chewing mushrooms, frequently reported on the welfare
of villagers who were in distant places. The Wassons
themselves received a description of the state of mind and
activities of their son Peter, who was thousands of miles

away in the United States. It seemed to the Wassons fantastic that anything they were told by this native could actually apply to their son so far away; but on their return home they were able to confirm that this clairvoyant report had been correct in every detail.

The Aztecs used peyote, and the modern Indians of the Native American Church have incorporated it into their culture, not for the kind of excitement that narcotics or alcohol produce, but for mystical experiences which are an integral part of their religion and their lives.

Recently, biochemists and pharmacologists, in trying to develop a cure for schizophrenia, have synthesized in their laboratories powerful new hallucinogenic drugs, such as mescaline and LSD 25 (lysergic acid diethylamide). The most minute quantities of these chemicals produce tremendous and long-lasting effects. Not by any means recommended for the use of the general public, these drugs in the hands of skilled doctors are opening up new realms for many. Psychologists are finding them useful in studying psychosis, in observing states of fear and anger, and in investigating the learning processes involved in conditioning and abstract thinking. When LSD is used in psychiatric analysis, stubborn layers of civilization and ego-defense are peeled off at once, and the patient, with the help of the psychiatrist, is often able to come to grips with his problems within a fairly short time.

Because they produce effects very similar to schizophrenia, hallucinogens must be used only under strict medical supervision. Usually the subject passes through a short spell of giddiness, nausea, and nervousness; and some people experience such frightening nightmares that it is necessary for the doctor to administer an antidote and bring them out at once. But others soon feel a heightened awareness, mystical and deeply spiritual.

The study of the mental manifestations as aided by the use of chemical substances has given us the word "psychedelics." Dr. Humphry Osmond of Canada was one of the pioneer researchers in psychedelics. In his report on hallucinogens issued in March, 1957 by the New York Academy of Sciences he says:

> Most subjects find the experience valuable, some find it frightening, and many say it is uniquely lovely. All, from . . . unsophisticated Indians to men of great learning, agree that much of it is beyond verbal description. Our subjects, who include . . . authors, artists, a junior cabinet minister, scientists, a hero, philosophers, and business men, are nearly all in agreement in this respect. For myself, my experiences with these substances have been the most strange, most awesome and among the most beautiful things in a fortunate and varied life. These are not escapes but enlargements, burgeonings of reality. In so far as I can judge, they occur . . . because the brain, although its functioning is impaired, acts more subtly and complexly than when it is normal. Yet surely when poisoned, the brain's actions should be less complex, rather than more so? I cannot argue about this because one must undergo the experience oneself. Those who have had these experiences know, and those who have not had them cannot know, and, what is more, the latter are in no position to offer a useful explanation.

A book published in 1961 called *Exploring Inner Space** is ascribed to Jane Dunlap, a pseudonym for a well-known writer in the field of nutrition. Her previous books have been persuasive enough to send thousands to the health food stores in search of Tiger's Milk; now her mental adventures under the influence of LSD have been related in just as compelling a manner.

Jane Dunlap saw visions of incomparable scope, and her insight was immeasurably heightened. She comprehended effortlessly many cosmic concepts which most people, even with deep soul-searching, have seldom been able to discern.

Aldous Huxley is another enchanted by his experiments with hallucinogens. He has said of them:* "This is how one ought to see—how things really are!"

*Essay: "The Doors of Perception."
*Harcourt, Brace & World, Inc., New York, 1961.

Parapsychologists are concerned with psychedelics to learn just this—how things really are. Less engrossed in the revelatory intensifications of the physical, their interest is the psychic. They hope that with supervised testing, the drugs will open up new doors to the secrets of extrasensory perception.

There is always the chance that psychic phenomena, mediumship, ESP, and visions may eventually be explained, at least partially, by chemical influences on the human mind and body; therefore psychical research of the future will make more and more use of hallucinogenic drugs. Eileen J. Garrett has lent herself to investigation in the effects of psychedelics, and she tells us* that she believes her LSD psychic experiences have made her a better, more accurate sensitive.

But extrasensory perception from hallucinogens is not limited to sensitives. Jane Dunlap relates a telepathic incident which occurred when she and a friend Helen took LSD. Under the influence of the drug, Helen was reliving an unhappy part of her early childhood. She had a compulsive urge to jump into the nearby swimming pool, although at that age she had been unable to swim. During this same time Jane was visioning her friend as a child of two. She became unbearably frightened that this young Helen would jump into the water and drown.

Dr. Andrija Puharich in *Beyond Telepathy** tells of a friend whom he calls Bob Rame, a forty-four-year-old highly successful New York business executive. This man learned to have hallucinogenic visions from inadvertently sniffing the ethyl ether content of cement he was using on a piece of plywood. Rame soon began to use this drug to make himself sleepy at night; then he found that he was having sensations of floating out of his body.

*"Psychopharmacological Parallels in Mediumship," *Proceedings* of Two Conferences on Parapsychology and Pharmacology, Parapsychology Foundation, Inc., New York, 1961.
*Doubleday & Co., Garden City, N. Y., 1962.

After that he began to travel about and observe many strange scenes. He found himself going through floors, ceilings, and walls, diving to the earth, and soaring high above the clouds. In about nine months he was able to have astral projections without needing the booster sniff of ethyl ether to get him off the ground.

A most astounding trip started in the same manner as others except that instead of merely floating upward, he seemed to be travelling rapidly through space. After what seemed a long time he found himself in a darkened theatre, and then later he discovered himself to be an ill person in a strange bed. Those standing about the bed were overjoyed when he opened his eyes. They helped him up, but he knew that he was not the person they thought he was, and he tried to tell them. Then, feeling his intrusion was not in the best taste, he "took-off" and was soon travelling on again as if he were in an aeroplane looking down at the earth.

A little later Rame awoke, this time in the body of a man who was so drunk that his companions were supporting him to walk. Aware that he must stop occupying other people's bodies, Rame made a special effort of will. From his diary the following excerpt indicates his reactions: "With this thought, I was again speeding through the blur, and I did this for what seemed a very long time. Then I opened my eyes and I was lying in my own bed. I sat up, smoked, and thought over the whole thing. I'm sure there is more but I could not recall all of it at this moment of writing. I decided that if this was a dream, it was totally unlike any I'd ever had before, and certainly didn't seem to have the characteristics of a dream; all places and people were unfamiliar to me, consciously at any rate. I speculated . . . that I simply was going around and invading bodies whose conscious mind is weak at the moment, thus permitting me to 'get in and out' due to this weakness. This was the most unusual 'non-inhalation' experience to date."

But an even more impressive and convincing non-inhalation episode was to come, for he endeavored to prove where he had been during his out-of-body visitation. He consciously attempted to drop in on two friends, Boris, who had been ill and in bed, and his wife Lomar. These persons lived on a hill, and as Rame began his travelling from the couch in his office he seemed to be going up a hill. He came upon Boris and Lomar outside their house. He was momentarily confused, because he had intended to visit Boris in his bedroom, where he was sure he would find his sick friend. Boris was dressed in a light overcoat and hat. Lomar wore dark clothes and coat.

Rame says: "They were coming toward me, so I stopped. They seemed in good spirits and walked past me unseeing in the direction of some building like a garage. I floated around in front of them, waving, trying to get their attention, without result."

Rame returned to his office, and later that day told his wife about what he thought he had seen. Then he called Boris and Lomar on the telephone, and, not telling them what he had done, asked where they were between four and five that afternoon. Lomar said that at roughly four twenty-five they were walking out of the house towards the garage. She was going to the post office, and Boris had decided that perhaps some fresh air might help him, and had dressed and gone along. When asked what they had been wearing Lomar stated that she wore a black skirt and a red sweater which was covered with a black car coat. Boris was wearing a light hat and a light coat.

It is interesting to note that this case which started out as an accidental reaction from a hallucinogen became a notable example of travelling clairvoyance. Travelling clairvoyance, or what was called apparitions of the living in the days of the Census of Hallucinations, is now more generally referred to as out-of-body experience or astral projection. Early mesmerists had discovered that some patients in hypnotic trance could be told to go travelling mentally. Then, while the body remained where it was and spoke of what the mind was seeing, the mind would seem to visit a designated place and report details about what was going on there, sometimes gathering information which was later verified.

An account of such a case was given in Mrs. Sidgwick's paper "On the Evidence for Clairvoyance."* A woman called Jane, the wife of a Durham pitman, was hypnotized at intervals for many years for the sake of her health, and while in trance she would ask to "travel"—to be guided by suggestion to places which she might clairvoyantly visit. Dr. F., who hypnotized her, tells us that he had informed one of his patients, Mr. Eglinton, that he would have Jane call upon him clairvoyantly in his home at Tynemouth, where, she, of course, had never been in person. Mr. Eglinton was just recovering from a very severe illness and was thin and weak.

The doctor had described to Jane the place he wanted her to visit. "Before us," he added, "we see a house with a laburnum tree in front of it."

She replied, "Is it the red house with a brass knocker?"

"No," said the doctor, "it has an iron knocker." (But he later learned that the knocker was brass.)

When it came time for her to describe the gentleman she was to visit, Jane stated that he was fat, not thin. She asked if he had a cork leg. She pictured him as sitting by the table with papers beside him and a glass of brandy and water. She told the doctor that his name was Eglinton, spelling it carefully. He writes: "I was so convinced that I had at last detected her in a complete mistake that I arose, and declined proceeding further in the matter, stating that, although her description of the house and the name of the person were correct, in everything connected with the gentleman she had guessed the opposite from the truth."

The doctor discovered the next day, however, that his friend's name Eglinton, which he had previously been in the habit of writing "Eglington," was correctly spelled as Jane had given it. He also learned that this gentleman had found himself unable to sit up so late, and so had ordered a figure to be formed of his clothes. To make the contrast more striking, he had had an extra pillow pushed under the waistcoat to "form a corporation." The dummy had been placed in a sitting position beside the table, on which were a glass of brandy and water and the newspapers.

Hypnosis as a factor in travelling clairvoyance is relatively infrequent. It more often occurs spontaneously. An individual under anaesthesia may suddenly find himself floating about near the ceiling of the room as he looks at his body lying inert upon the operating table, or, as already noted, these projections may occur to people who are just relaxing. But more frequently they happen in times of crisis.

Sir Auckland Geddes in an address before the Royal Society of Medicine on February 26, 1927 told of a recent out-of-body experience which happened to him. He had begun to feel very ill one midnight when alone and by two o'clock was definitely suffering from acute gastroenteritis. By the next morning his pulse and respiration became quite impossible to count, he wanted to ring for assistance, but was unable to, and so "quite placidly gave up the attempt," he tells us. "I realized I was very ill and very quickly reviewed my whole financial position. Thereafter at no time did my consciousness appear to me to

173

be in any way dimmed." But he suddenly realized that his consciousness was separating from another consciousness which was also his. His ego, or the consciousness which was now him, seemed to be altogether outside of his body, which it could see. "Gradually," he said, "I realized that I could see, not only my body, and the bed it was in, but everything in the whole house and garden, and then realized that I was seeing not only 'things' at home, but in London and in Scotland, in fact wherever my attention was directed, it seemed to me; and the explanation which I received, from what source I do not know, but which I found myself calling my mentor, was that I was free in a time-dimension of space, where 'now' was in some way equivalent to 'here' in the ordinary three-dimensional space of everyday life.

"I saw someone enter my bedroom; I realized she got a terrible shock and I saw her hurry to the telephone. I saw my doctor leave his patients and come very quickly, and heard him say, or saw him think, 'he is nearly gone.' I heard him quite clearly speaking to me on the bed, but I was not in touch with my body and could not answer him. I was really cross when he took his syringe and rapidly injected my body with something which I afterwards learned was camphor. As the heart began to beat more strongly, I was drawn back, and I was intensely annoyed, because I was so interested and just beginning to understand where I was and what I was 'seeing.' I came back into the body really angry at being pulled back, and once I was back, all the clarity of vision of anything and everything disappeared and I was just possessed of a glimmer of consciousness, which was suffused with pain."*

In the following case it will be noted that veridical information was brought back from a similar out-of-body experience. The writer knows a woman in her staid and

*G.N.M. Tyrrell, *The Personality of Man*, Pelican Books, Baltimore, 1948, pp. 197-98.

sensible seventies who nearly died when she was a young
girl. While she was comatose, scarcely breathing, she de-
clares, her conscious mind seemed to be floating up in the
air . . . up, up, until she could look far below at her body
on the bed with her family gathered anxiously around
the doctor administering to her. Accompanying her on her
flight—her pilot, as it were, or navigator—was a man
she did not know. He told her his name was Edison Prescott, the last name being the same as her doctor's.

As this girl saw her mother praying desperately for her
recovery she felt that she must return to her physical
body, and she did. When she was conscious again she
asked her doctor if he knew someone named Edison
Prescott. Startled from his professional composure, he
said, "Why, that's my brother who died many years ago.
How did you know his name? I've never mentioned him
to you."

The previous examples may be ascribed to the crisis
of critical illness; yet sometimes astral projections seem
so pointless as to be unexplainable by any reasonable
hypothesis. The following incident* could only be interpreted as an "arrival" case, where the man's mind was so
fixed on his return that his image preceded him. Major
William M. Bigge writes of what happened to him while
quartered in Templemore, County Tipperary. One afternoon he distinctly saw Lt. Col. Reed walk toward the
mess hall and go in the door. Reed was dressed in a brown
shooting jacket, with grey summer regulation tweed trou-
sers, and had a fishing rod and a landing net in his hand.
As the incident occurred in February, Major Bigge was
surprised to see his brother officer with fishing gear in
such a costume. He had never seen him so outfitted before.

Major Bigge, wishing to speak to the Colonel, followed
him into the building, only to find that he had disap-

*Phantasms of the Living, Vol. II, p. 94.

peared and had not been seen by anyone inside. After searching all about, Major Bigge, now in the barrack-yard, was speaking to several others of Colonel Reed's strange disappearance. At that moment they all saw the Colonel walk into the barrack-yard through the gate, which was in the opposite direction from the mess hall. He was in precisely the identical dress in which Bigge had seen him and had a rod and landing net in his hand. He had been fishing, a very unusual thing to do at that time of year, and had been out for more than two hours. He had not been near the mess hall since morning.

There have been instances where more than one person has been seen simultaneously out of body, and where more than one person has seen them. The Reverend W. Mountford of Boston, Massachusetts told of such a case.*

One day Mountford was visiting some friends in Norfolk, and he stood at the window looking up the road. "Here is your brother and his wife coming," he said. His host and hostess both looked, too, and said, "Yes, and look, he has old Dobbin out again," referring to a horse who was just recovering from an accident. The people in the buggy, whom they could plainly see, passed by the house, and turned the corner and disappeared. Everyone was shocked that they should not have stopped in.

A few moments later a young lady entered, pale and excited. "Oh, aunt!" she exclaimed, "I have had such a fright! Father and mother have passed me on the road without speaking." Her parents had looked straight ahead and never stopped nor said a word. When she had left home not fifteen minutes before, they had been sitting by the fire, and now they drove by her without speaking, yet she was certain they had seen her.

While everyone was still discussing the contretemps, the Reverend Mountford looked out the window once

*Phantasms of the Living, Vol. II, p. 97.

again and saw the same scene reenacted, although this time the man and wife stopped and came in. They declared that they had not passed previously, having been at home until ten minutes before, when they had started their ride.

A more recent case of this type is given us by Harold Sherman,* the sensitive on the receiving end of Sir Hubert Wilkins' Arctic adventures. He had a friend in California named Harry J. Loose. On Thanksgiving Day, 1941, when Sherman came in to the Canterbury Apartments in Hollywood, where he lived, the desk clerk handed him a memorandum slip. It read: "Mr. Loose was here—will see you Sunday."

Plans had already been made for the Shermans to visit the Looses on Sunday, and Sherman had not expected Loose to be in Hollywood that day. Sherman immediately called his friend at his home in Monterey Park and expressed regret for having missed him. Loose replied, "Harold, there's been some mistake. You have me confused with someone else. I didn't come to see you. I haven't been out of the house today."

Then Sherman checked with the desk clerk, William A. Cousins, and received an exact description of Harry Loose, even to the clothes which he was wearing—which turned out to be the identical clothes he had worn that day in Monterey Park where he was spending the holiday with his wife and family. As Sherman later learned, Loose had been napping at the time that the clerk saw him come into the apartment house lobby, look about vaguely, and then ask for Sherman and leave the message.

A few days later Sherman and Loose tested the clerk, to see if he would recognize the gentleman of the apparition when he appeared in the flesh. As Sherman hid, Loose walked through the lobby and up to the desk.

You Live After Death, Fawcett Publications, Inc., New York, 1956.

"Good afternoon, Mr. Loose," said Cousins, who afterwards wrote his testimony to the experience, saying that it was the most thrilling happening of his life to have been involved in such a singular episode.

Occasionally astral projection occurs in a dream. In the following instance the percipient believed herself to be dreaming, yet she was seen by her mother in a distant place.*

A young woman who calls herself Martha Johnson, twenty-six years old, single, and living several hundred miles from her mother, dreamed on the night of January 26, 1957 that she was particularly angry about something and wished to tell her mother. She seemed to be walking in her dream, eventually going through considerable blackness at what seemed to be a great height. Then all at once she could see a small bright oasis of light down below her and she knew it was the house where her mother lived. Her account goes on: "After I entered, I leaned up against the dish cupboard with folded arms, a pose I often assume. I looked at my mother who was bending over something white and doing something with her hands. She did not appear to see me at first, but she finally looked up. I had a sort of pleased feeling and then after standing a second more, I turned and walked about four steps."

Then Miss Johnson seemed enveloped in a mist, and at this point she woke up. She looked at her bedside clock and noted the time to be 2:10 A.M. She did not write to her mother about her dream, but in a few days received a letter from her which stated in part:

"You [have said in the past that you can't sleep,] well, why don't you stay home and not go gallivanting so far from home when you do sleep? Did you know you were here for a few seconds? I believe it was Saturday night, 1:10, . . It would have been 10 after 2 your time. I was pressing a blouse here in the kitchen—I couldn't sleep either. I looked up and there you were by the cupboard just standing smiling at me. I started to speak and saw you were gone. . . . It's a terribly lonely feeling when you go like that—you could at least have said something. Did you dream?"

Miss Johnson's mother had seen her twice previously, as she apparently has travelled in her dreams on other occasions.

Besides being a dream case, the above also illustrates the reciprocal nature of some out-of-body experiences. The agent is aware of his astral travelling and is also seen at the place where he believes himself to have visited. An instance with historical interest occurred when Alfonso di Liguori in 1774 was in prison at Arezzo, fasting. On awakening one morning, he stated that he had been at the bedside of the dying Pope Clement XIV. Investigation revealed that he had actually been seen by those present at the Pope's bedside.

Perhaps the most curious story of reciprocal travelling clairvoyance ever to be reported is the Wilmot case, also given in Mrs. Sidgwick's paper "On the Evidence for Clairvoyance."

Mr. S. R. Wilmot, a manufacturer of Bridgeport, Connecticut, sailed on October 3, 1863 from Liverpool for New York on the steamer *City of Limerick,* accompanied by his sister, Miss Eliza E. Wilmot. There were terrible storms during the first days of the trip, and on the ninth night Mr. Wilmot had his first refreshing sleep since leaving port.

"Toward morning," he reports, "I dreamed that I saw my wife, whom I had left in the United States, come to the door of my state room, clad in her night dress. At the door she seemed to discover that I was not the only occupant of the room, hesitated a little, then advanced to my side, stooped down and kissed me, and after gently caressing me for a few moments, quietly withdrew.

"Upon waking I was surprised to see my fellow-passenger,

whose berth was above mine, but not directly over it—owing to the fact that our room was at the stern of the vessel—leaning upon his elbow, and looking fixedly at me. 'You're a pretty fellow,' said he at length, 'to have a lady come and visit you in this way.' I pressed him for an explanation, which he at first declined to give, but at length related what he had seen while wide awake, lying in his berth. It exactly corresponded with my dream."

This gentleman was William J. Tait, a sedate 50-year-old man who was most impressed by what he had seen. He told Miss Wilmot about it the next morning. In fact, he asked her if it was she who had come into the room. She was naturally quite taken aback at the query.

Mr. Wilmot continues: "The day after landing I went by rail to Watertown, Connecticut, where my children and my wife had been for some time, visiting her parents. Almost her first question when we were alone together was, 'Did you receive a visit from me a week ago Tuesday?' 'A visit from you?' said I. 'We were more than a thousand miles at sea.' 'I know it,' she replied, 'but it seemed to me that I visited you.' 'It would be impossible,' said I. 'Tell me what makes you think so' "

His wife then told him that on account of the severity of the weather she had been extremely anxious about him. On the night in question she had lain awake for a long time thinking of him, and about four o'clock in the morning it seemed to her that she went out to seek him. Crossing the wide and stormy sea, she came at length to a low, black steamship, whose side she went up. Then, descending into the cabin, she passed through it to the stern until she came to his stateroom.

"Tell me," she said, "do they ever have staterooms like the one I saw, where the upper berth extends further back than the under one? A man was in the upper berth, looking right at me, and for a moment I was afraid to go in, but soon I went up to the side of your berth, bent down and kissed you, and embraced you, and then went away."

The description given by Mrs. Wilmot of the steamship was correct in all particulars, though she had never seen it.

Although this delicious example would seem to be a three-way stretch of the imagination, it was thoroughly verified. It shows once again how travellers on the magic carpet of astral projection may return with extrasensory information. Another occurred when the Reverend L. J. Bertrand, a Huguenot minister, found himself contemplating his frozen body on a mountain peak in the Alps.

He had sat down on a ledge to await the return of the students and guide who had accompanied him on the climb, and now his body was solidly immovable. He had felt himself becoming gradually frozen, from his toes upward. Eventually his head was unbearably cold, and then there was a brief moment of such intense pain that Bertrand thought he must surely have died. After that he had seemed to escape out of the top of his head like a ball of air, a captive balloon, still attached to the body by a kind of elastic string.

The Reverend Bertrand thought about the rest of his party, and this balloon in which his mind now existed caught up with them. It watched as they made wrong turns, against his previous instructions, and got lost, and as the guide sat down behind a rock and ate *his*, Bertrand's, lunch.

Then he turned his attention to his wife, who had planned to join him in Lucerne three days hence. As he watched, he saw her arrive at the hotel in Lucerne in a carriage with four others. About this time the guide and students returned from their climb, and found him, as they thought, dead.

"Poor young friends," he mused, "they do not know that I never was as alive as I am now." But the guide began to rub his body with snow, and eventually he came reluctantly to himself. When he then charged the students with taking the wrong path, and the guide with making free with his chicken and wine, they were amazed and frightened. Even his wife, as she might well have been, was disconcerted when he met her in Lucerne and informed her that she had arrived two days early in a carriage with four other people.

"Who told you all that?" she asked. "Did you have someone spying on me?"

"Certainly not," replied the Reverend, laughing smugly. He felt very happy about his entire experience. As far as he was concerned he had now confirmed what he had been preaching to his congregations all the years of his ministry. He now believed with certainty that there is something which survives death.

W. E. Woodward, in his autobiography *The Gift of Life,* tells of an episode related to him by American novelist Theodore Dreiser. Dreiser said he had been entertaining the English writer John Cowper Powys who had to leave rather early. When he left he said, "I'll appear before you, right here, later this evening. You'll see me." Dreiser, chuckling at Powys' whimsy, asked if he was going to turn himself into a ghost. Powys said, "I don't know yet. I may return as a spirit or in some other astral form."

As he sat reading several hours later, Dreiser looked up and there he saw Powys, who looked exactly as natural as he had in person a short time before, except that "A pale light glow shone from the figure." When Dreiser spoke and moved toward him, the apparition vanished.

This is another instance where an individual tries to make himself seen at a distant place, as was observed in the case of the brash Mr. S. H. Beard. But exactly what purpose does this power serve beyond diverting one's friends or capering nimbly in a lady's chamber?

Well, those who have undergone such out-of-body experience, in any of its variations, consider it to be impressive evidence that human consciousness is separable from the body and therefore can exist independently from it. This leads them to believe that at death something similar occurs: the body dies and the mind, or consciousness continues to live.

Frederic W. H. Myers says that "In these self-projections we have before us, I do not say the most useful, but the most extraordinary achievement of the human will. What can lie further outside any known capacity than the power to cause a semblance of oneself to appear at a distance? What can be a more central action—more manifestly the outcome of whatsoever is deepest and most unitary in man's whole being? . . . Other achievements have their manifest limit; where is the limit here?" The spirit has shown itself as if in part dissociated from the body; to what point may its dissociation go? The spirit has shown some independence, some intelligence, some permanence. To what degree of intelligence, independence, permanence, then, may it conceivably attain? "Of all vital phenomena, I say, this is the most significant; this self-projection is the one definite act which it seems as though a man might perform equally well before and after bodily death."

14 *The Future of ESP*

NOW, MYERS WAS A
poet, and although he certainly became a hard-core scientist before he finished with his psychical research, he always retained his interest and delight in "the strange and wonderful upper stories of man's soul house." To him proof that man can survive bodily death was the great goal of psychical research. To him it was curious that so little attention was paid to a prospect of such intense importance. In his Introduction to *Human Personality and Its Survival of Bodily Death* he said in effect that, in the long story of man's endeavors to understand his own environment and to govern his own fate, there is one gap or omission so singular that its simple statement has the air of a paradox. Yet it is strictly true to say that man has never yet applied the methods of modern science to the problem which most profoundly concerns him—whether or not his personality involves any element which can survive bodily death.

But, Myers continues, neither those who believe on vague grounds or those who believe on definite grounds that the question might possibly be solved by human observation of objective fact have made any serious attempt in this direction. They have not sought for fresh corroborative instances, for analogies, for explanations; rather they have kept their convictions on these fundamental matters in a separate and sealed compartment of their minds, a compartment consecrated to religion or to superstition, but not to observation or experiment.

The purpose of Myers' book, and the great objective of the Society for Psychical Research, was to do what could be done to break down that artificial wall between science and what has been called superstition. Myers' primary contention is that in the discussion of the deeper problems of man's nature and destiny there ought to be exactly the same openness of mind, diligence in the search for objective evidence of any kind, and critical analysis of results as is habitually shown, for instance, in the discussion of the nature and destiny of the planet upon which man now moves.

This was said in 1900, and it holds true today. We are still as hesitant as we ever have been to investigate scientifically the possibility of our survival of bodily death. It is perhaps the very fact that psychical research includes a consideration of evidence for survival that has made science so reluctant to admit it into the sacred halls of systematized knowledge.

The difficulty even to get a hearing if one admits belief in survival over and beyond religious faith, is pointed out by Dr. S. Ralph Harlow, retired professor of Religion at Smith College, and ordained minister of the Congregational Church.

"Under normal circumstances," he says, "I am considered a . . . reliable witness. Attorneys have solicited my testimony, and I have testified in the courts, regarded by judge and jury as dependable and honest."

Yet Dr. Harlow finds that when he relates his experiences with the little understood phenomena of psychical research, his testimony is frequently questioned. He does not let this discourage him from affirming that he actually has been a witness to phenomena which he believes to be conclusive evidence of survival.

Eleanor Sidgwick was for over fifty years one of the most active, diligent, and objective workers in the S.P.R. During that time she never once stated her position on the question of survival. In fact, in her published accounts of her observations and her investigations it was frequently felt by some of her associates that the note of caution and reserve had been, if possible, even over-emphasized. However, when her paper on the first half century of the Society was presented by her brother Lord Balfour at its Jubilee meeting, July 1, 1932, Balfour stated, with Mrs. Sidgwick's permission, her conclusions after her extensive and prolonged study of the psychic. He said: "I have Mrs. Sidgwick's assurance that, upon the evidence before her, she herself is a firm believer both in survival and in the reality of communication between the living and the dead." This belief, said Lord Balfour, he himself had come to share.

The position for the defense has been summed up most succinctly by Brigadier C.A.L. Brownlow, who says: "Psychics is one name for that great range of human experience, attested to by men down the ages, that points to the truth of survival . . . It is important because it is the only evidence we have of life after death."

However, for the purposes of this book, it doesn't really matter whether one believes in survival or not. What is under scrutiny is extrasensory perception; and extrasensory perception may be the alternative to communication with a personalized hereafter. If, as we have discussed, mediums do not receive their information from spirits, or perform through their intervention, then the medium's faculty must certainly come from some other extrasensory, supernormal source.

ESP is not super*natural* in the implied sense of "spooky," "magical," "mysterious," or anything involving the co-operation of spiritual or diabolical agencies. ESP is super*normal,* meaning that it is beyond what we at present accept as normal, subject to established natural laws. Someday, when we discover still more about natural laws, ESP will fall into line.

This prospect naturally induces speculations as to its usefulness and potentialities, were ESP to become universally active. Eric Dingwall and John Langdon-Davies extend extrasensory perception to an ultimate conclusion which has truly uncomfortable implications. They say:*

> Just imagine what life would be if telepathy were a common, everyday affair. For good or for evil alike, our present way of living would stop. Our everyday conventions are based on the very fact that ESP does *not* exist, that secrets can be kept, that ordinary ways of imparting information have to be used. Nine-tenths of our material civilization would become senseless if anybody could get in touch with anybody else by way of ESP. But not only nine-tenths of our material civilization; our very way of thinking and feeling would be completely altered. Every action inspired by love or hate, our needs for self-preservation, all our relations with other human beings would become futile, if with ESP in general use we tried to carry on as at present.
>
> You might think that if ESP were general we should know more than we do and be able to have an even more advanced civilization than we have; but that is precisely what would not have happened. If we had continued to exercise ESP (supposing it once to have been well-nigh universal), we would never have learned to use our eyes as we have had to, we would never have developed science and logical thought, which depend on training our eyes and mental processes to find out unknown things; we would, in fact, have remained content with a very limited world and a very limited use of our brains. In short, man would not have risen in the scale of evolution and his social evolution would not have taken the line it has done, had he retained the habit of using ESP. For ESP is a handicap to the kind of logical thought on which human progress has been built.

Fortunately, and in the face of such graphic sweeping comment, no one expects ESP to assume such King Kong proportions. Even were ESP to become embarrassingly widespread, however, it is to be presumed that our civilization would ultimately adapt itself to encompass it.

Another view somewhat different is that of Harold Sherman, who believes that "recognition of the laws behind the operation of ESP and knowledge of how to bring these higher powers of mind under conscious directional

*In *The Unknown—Is It Nearer?*

control, are going to be the next great steps in man's upward progress. True knowledge of mind, of his own inner self—with man's faith supported by the findings of science —will do more eventually to bring about the centuries-old dream of universal brotherhood than any other intelligent force. We cannot understand our fellow man, nor he us, until we have come closer to solving the mystery of our own selves, our relation to each other, and to this universe."

This is amplified by Dr. Rhine's statement* that, "Our feelings for men depend on our ideas, our knowledge, about them. The more we are led on the one hand to think of our fellow men as deterministic, physical systems—robots, machines, brains—the more heartlessly and selfishly we can allow ourselves to deal with them. On the other hand, the more we appreciate their mental life as something unique in nature, something more original and creative than the mere space-time-mass relations of matter, the more we are interested in them as individuals, and the more we tend to respect them and consider their viewpoints and feelings. Our interpersonal dealings are elevated to a level of mutual interest, of understanding, of fellowship.

"It is no mere historic accident that those systems of belief which have most dignified man with properties beyond the physical are the ones which have also built up the loftiest appreciation and esteem of man for man, the highest development of fraternal regard. Therefore, anything that supports this psychocentric conception of man with reliable knowledge would manifestly be underwriting a basis for happier relations in human society."

Does extrasensory perception, then, support the concept of man as a spiritual as well as a physical entity? It would

*The Reach of the Mind, p. 219.

seem to. And isn't something which can do man this service worth struggling to advance? It has been a long, hard fight and the way ahead stretches endlessly. Yet perhaps the biggest step has already been taken. "Certainly," as Dingwall and Langdon-Davies affirm, "no unprejudiced person can any longer deny the rank of science to psychical research. Certain phenomena have been repeatedly observed under sound laboratory conditions, and unless somebody can disprove all the results, paranormal phenomena . . . must be accepted as certainly as the other facts of natural science. The Unknown has been taken by its unseen hand and courteously but firmly led into the science laboratory."

So with ESP well on its way, we leave it, frank to admit that beyond the vague suggestion that it is a vestigial trait, we don't know why or what it is, only that it does exist. Can it be developed, produced at will and controlled, or must it remain a fleeting, evasive, tantalizing enigma?

There are endless possibilities for future exploration. And aren't we glad there are new frontiers of inner as well as outer space for us eventually to conquer?

THE END